To Clarissa,
Keep trusting in God's
unfailing love!

Eva Marie Dyke
I Cor. 3:18, NIV

FOREWORD BY WILLIAM M. PINSON JR.

REFLECTIONS
ON GOD'S
Grace
AND OTHER THEMES

MED... ...LK WITH GOD

...OYKE

For

Clarissa

REFLECTIONS ON
GOD'S GRACE AND GLORY
AND OTHER THEMES
BY EVA MARIE DYKE

MEDITATIONS FOR A DEEPER WALK WITH GOD

REFLECTIONS ON GOD'S *Grace* AND *Glory* AND OTHER THEMES

BY

Eva Marie Dyke

A Prayer

Be still, my soul, and listen to the whisperings of the Holy Spirit.
He is murmuring assurances of God's unfailing love and His abundant mercies.
He is rekindling your spiritual fires and illuminating Jesus.

Dear Father,
help this child of Yours to heed the Good Shepherd's callings,
to follow wherever He leads,
and to rest in the adequacy of His grace
even when the terrain is rugged and earthly strengths are waning.

May the ears of Your servant always
be eager to respond to Your loving commands—
knowing Your divine intention is to transform her
into a glorious reflection of Your Son, the Lord Jesus Christ.

"And we, who with unveiled faces all reflect the Lord's glory,
are being transformed into his likeness with ever-increasing glory,
which comes from the Lord, who is the Spirit."
(2 CORINTHIANS 3:18)

TABLE OF CONTENTS

FOREWORD

William M. Pinson Jr.

This collection of meditations entitled *Reflections on God's Grace and Glory* is appropriately named. Furthermore, the author has done what few could do.

These inspiring devotionals are indeed reflections. The great complex issues of the Christian faith are dealt with, such as the nature of God, Jesus Christ, creation, salvation, and prayer, in a way that reflects aspects of the subject but does not plumb its depths. Make no mistake, the author could plumb each one deeply; she is a highly educated Bible scholar and experienced theologian. However, in these pages she chooses not to elaborate on these but rather to reflect sparkling truths that reside in each.

As such this book likely ought to be read not as a Bible study, devotional book, theological treatise, or autobiography, although in a sense it is all of these, but as a series of brief devotionals to be read thoughtfully, each page prayerfully pondered as a separate beautiful reflection. These meditations could well be read aloud in a group setting but somehow they seem to fit more into a quiet, individual devotional time.

Few persons have the life ingredients to pen reflections such as these. A Bible professor with graduate degrees in her field, including an earned doctorate from an accredited seminary, she does not endeavor to display her knowledge but rather to communicate truth in a way all persons can understand and apply to life. An ardent student in the field of world religions she maintains an unwavering commitment to Jesus Christ as Lord while sharing with persons of other faiths why she holds that singular commitment. A world traveler with wide friendships around the globe she relates to strangers with compassion that indeed reflects that of her Lord.

All of these ingredients you will discover in the following pages and in discovering them realize that indeed few persons possess all of the experiences and attributes that make the reflections possible. The brief biographical word that follows may help to explain how she came to acquire such an amazing array of skills and experiences.

My friendship with this talented person goes back many decades. I was active as a student in the Baptist ministry program of one state university when she was the director of such a program in another state university across the city. Therefore I did not first come to know her as a director but as a member of the church to which we both belonged. She frequently brought devotionals and shared stories in various meetings of the church and I marveled then as I do now at her ability to convey deep truth in simple ways, to communicate compassion without maudlin sentimentality, and to use the English language in as beautiful a fashion as anyone I had ever known.

Through the years she continued to minister to students, to teach the Bible, and to maintain a strong interest in internationals. Her ministry with international students took her to posts literally coast to coast, serving as Director of International Ministries with the Home Mission Board of the Southern Baptist Convention in the San Francisco Bay Area with a major focus on the University of California at Berkeley during the tumultuous sixties and early seventies and then as Director of International Ministries in the Mt. Vernon Baptist Association in northern Virginia. In these places she taught, directed retreats, entertained internationals in her home, and shared Christ with persons who had come to America from literally all over the world and from all religions. For eighteen years she taught Bible and world religions as an instructor at Temple College in Temple, Texas. In addition she has served as adjunct professor in several colleges and seminaries.

She married Paul Thomas Dyke, PhD, whose career as an agricultural research scientist with a major university has taken him to developing nations throughout the world. Their marriage has been ministry focused. Often in their travels they shared their faith in Christ and fellowshipped with Christians from various cultures as well as missionaries serving in those places. They met individuals during these travels with whom they have maintained a meaningful, sustained relationship.

The Dykes in retirement continue to relate to internationals, primarily by inviting them into their home for a meal and dialogue. As personal needs surface with these persons from many cultures and religions the Dykes seek to minister to those needs. This ministry is one means of keeping a portion of their marriage vows: *"May our love also extend beyond ourselves to those less fortunate in the world—the lonely, the needy, and the broken."* Because of this loving care for others, although they have no biological children, they have many spiritual sons and daughters.

Church has always played a key role with the Dykes. He is a deacon and choir member. She teaches Bible studies and gives interpretative readings and messages to churches of many denominations.

Her ministries and abilities have been widely recognized. Awards and honors from many organizations have been bestowed on her. Her skills as a writer have been sought for various publications. A magnificent wordsmith, she pens phrases that sparkle on the page in keeping with the theme of this book—***reflections.***

Through the years I have known the author of this inspirational book by many names, such as Eva Marie at first, then as Dr. Eva Marie Kennard, then as Dr. Eva Marie Kennard Dyke, but she has remained the person I knew when first I met her, a brilliant, communicative, compassionate, humble, devout Christian woman. Thus the insights shared in these reflections come from first-hand life experiences.

I have benefited from the reflections found herein and believe you will also and am honored that the author allowed me to share some information about her that hopefully will add to your understanding of why she could "reflect" in such a beautiful, helpful fashion.

WILLIAM M. PINSON JR.
MAY 2012

Reflections!

RUINS OF THE 13TH CENTURY AUGUSTINIAN NUNNERY ON THE ISLE OF IONA, SCOTLAND

I am especially appreciative of the countless hours that Paul, my husband, devoted to this project. He plunged through "volumes" of photo books and stacks of slides made during our travels in order to find appropriate pictures to accompany my meditations.

DEDICATION

This book is dedicated to my husband Paul, "my lover, my friend," for forty years. He has been my great encourager, my sounding board, and my constant prodder. I am grateful for his patience and the way he practices listening love.

A valentine poem I penned for him many moons ago appears on the opposite page.

I would also like to dedicate this book to our many spiritual children including the McBeth family, Audine, Dennis and Roy; our Chinese daughter and grandson, Angela and Jonathan; our Nepali sons, Hari Dallakoti and Sudip Tiwari; our Chinese son, Kuodi Jian; our Ethiopian son, Bez Kebede; and others who have touched our lives and given us extraordinary joy and countless blessings.

EXPRESSIONS OF GRATITUDE

My earnest thanks go to Dr. Bill Pinson (former professor, pastor, seminary president, and currently Executive Director Emeritus for the Baptist General Convention of Texas), for his emotional support and spiritual guidance. His practical suggestions for improving my manuscript were gladly heeded. I have cherished his friendship for more than fifty years and rejoiced in his dedication to many Kingdom causes.

I also desire to express my gratitude to Debbie Manning Sheppard, Graphic Artist, who worked patiently with us to decide on the design and layout of this book. Her expertise and warm Christian spirit delighted our souls.

This one must also praise God for bringing Anita Majors (Brockell) to serve with her on the University of California, Berkeley campus. Our struggles and tears, our victories and spiritual rewards, as we ministered to international students during the turbulent sixties, bonded us together for life.

Love INSPIRED

God-bequeathed companion, whisper in my ear
That sweet dogma I delight to hear,
Assurances that my wifely frailties do not mar
Our devotion, God-renewed at every sunrise altar.

Tell me, ever honest soul,
That our togetherness, like a stole
Wraps a shivering, lonely world
As the Father's warmth in us unfurls.

Innocent convicter of my heart,
Keep believing in my better days,
Touch the inner me, share this soul's deep yearnings,
Hand in hand, our souls to follow God's determinings.

Playmate of my laughs, my every game,
Comfort in my hours of tears and shame,
Let me feel your care, share your load
Else life's for naught—why our abode?

Show me, listener to His footfall,
That every dream's according to God's call,
That each new day summons to a higher peak,
His amens, His blessings, for'er to seek.

Slayer of dragons, my noble knight,
Some day battles no more you'll fight;
Resurrection chimes ring! Come, my mate,
Our last journey—to heaven's open gate.

NOTE: *A valentine message to Paul from his loving wife, "Eve."*

ON THE WALLS IN MEDIEVAL DUBROVNIK, CROATIA

PREFACE

*M*y precious Daddy, who lived to the ripe old age of 99, was an amazing person who had multiple talents and spiritual gifts. He delighted in painting beautiful landscapes with his oils. He played any tune on the harmonica that he had ever heard, but he especially enjoyed playing hymns to accompany me as I "tickled the ivory."

But his passion (especially in his golden years) was his creative writing hobby. He composed poetry, essays, proverbs, and short stories. Although ten of his poems were published in an Anthology of American Poets, his primary desire was to pass these little gems on to his family and close friends.

Now I, as an octogenarian, want to follow in his footsteps. My little book of **Reflections on God's Grace and Glory** is intended for the same category of recipients. I pray my meditations will be a source of inspiration and challenge to those kind souls who decide to read them.

Some of the devotional thoughts mention international friends with whom I have had a meaningful ministry and an in-depth gospel witness. Since our marriage my husband, Paul, has likewise been involved in this outreach to Hindus, Buddhists, Muslims, and Christians from many lands.

In our marriage vows which we quoted at our wedding ceremony were these words, *"May our love also extend beyond ourselves to those less fortunate in the world—the needy, the lonely, and the broken."* We have tried with God's help to keep this vow.

EVA MARIE DYKE

Eva Marie Dyke, enjoying God's reflection
on CASTLE LAKE, COLORADO.
Just one of her inspirational trips
as she listens to God's still small voice . . . .

I pray my meditations

will be a source of inspiration

and challenge to

those kind souls

who decide to read them.

—Eva Marie

("Eve")

God's
ABIDING
Hope

When we earthlings place our hope in the transient things this world has to offer, we are often disappointed or disillusioned. Paul tells us in his letter to the ROMANS (5:5) that the kind of hope God gives to His children does not vanish when the storms rage and the usual "security blankets" are gone. This is because the Lord keeps pouring out His love into our hearts, and we possess a hope that never disappoints even in the darkest nights of the soul.

---

*WE POSSESS A HOPE
THAT NEVER DISAPPOINTS
EVEN IN THE DARKEST
NIGHTS OF THE SOUL.*

The Scripture tells us again and again that when we are downcast or disturbed about any situation in our lives, we are simply to put our hope in God (PSALM 42:11). But many people suffer one of the greatest afflictions known to humankind—hopelessness. Why? They continue to place their confidence, their trust, in the unstable, unreliable "gods" of this world. When the economy plummets they lose hope, when someone else gets the promotion at work they lose hope, when the congratulations and awards go to the less deserving they lose hope—and on and on go the woes.

Remember Job? Even during his deepest agony he clung tenaciously to his trust in God. His trials never smashed all of his hope (JOB 19:25).

Authentic prophets of God have always been heckled and harassed. Even today we can hear the "voices of the martyrs" as they are suffering the taunts and tortures of the ungodly. But ah! Their testimonies of faith and devotion to their King, the Lord Jesus, assure us they are forever clinging to their God-bestowed hope. They know, whatever happens, it is a win-win situation. They are shouting victoriously with the Apostle Paul, *"For to me, to live is Christ and to die is gain"* (PHILIPPIANS 1:21).

Can you persevere in faith even when the "sores" are oozing in your life or some of the persons dearest to you are hurling stones at you? You most assuredly can if you never surrender your hope to the Enemy. He only peddles a pseudo-hope that will eventually shrivel your soul. The kind of hope that God wants to give you will sustain you, stabilize you, and strengthen you.

Where are you placing your hope? *"My hope is built on nothing less than Jesus' blood and righteousness. I dare not trust the sweetest frame but wholly lean on Jesus' name. On Christ the solid Rock I stand. All other ground is sinking sand"* (HYMN: "THE SOLID ROCK").

*"...they [the Israelites during their
wilderness wanderings]
drank from the spiritual rock
that accompanied them,
and that rock was Christ."*
(1 CORINTHIANS 10:4B)

MONUMENT VALLEY, NEVADA >

God's
ALL-SEEING
Eye

When I was a little girl, my precious maternal Grandmother informed me one day (with a wee bit of severity in her voice) about God's All-Seeing Eye. Of course, after that revelation, I would not dare slip a cookie out of that special jar in her cupboard because that humongous Eye would sound an alarm. My misdemeanor would then be broadcast to everyone in the household.

How times have changed! Ever since as a young teenager I met this One who is omniscient, the inescapable Eye I once feared to offend has become my welcomed guardian.

I am reminded of my Persian friend, a professing Muslim who did not actually practice his faith. One day when we were eating together in the university dining hall he said, "Eva, the way you talk about this Jesus He could be sitting right here beside us. Frankly, I would be quite miserable if I thought I was perpetually being watched by some invisible God. I like my god where he is—far, far away; and he never interferes

with my personal life." Immediately I responded, "Oh, Moshtehedi, you think this way because you don't know Jesus. In love He is watching over me, desiring to keep me at my best. And I am grateful."

My international student friend merely shook his head and muttered, "That's interesting, Eva. But I like my independence too much to allow this Jesus of yours to invade my privacy."

Moshtehedi's response echoed my childhood fears of the All-Seeing Eye of God. Today, however, I live with a conscious awareness that He is watching over me with His loving, caring "Eyes." That is cause not for a moan but for authentic gratitude.

"For the eyes of the Lord range throughout the earth to strengthen those whose hearts are fully committed to him."
(2 CHRONICLES 16:9A)

^ *BAPTISTRY OF SANTA MARIA, FLORENCE, ITALY*

God's AWESOME Celebration

What was God's purpose when He created us? I believe we were meant to be in spiritual friendship with God, always celebrating His glory. But the Apostle Paul tells us in his letter to the Roman Christians, *"for all have sinned (missed the mark) and fall short of the glory of God"* (ROMANS 3:23). We have failed miserably to realize God's wonderful dream for us because we have not acknowledged His lordship over us.

What is the root sin? It is "me-ism." This disease has been afflicting humankind ever since the days of Adam and Eve. *"We all, like sheep have gone astray, each of us has turned to his own way…"* (ISAIAH 53:6A).

Paul's letter to the Ephesians reveals a world in which there is disharmony, disunity, and alienation from God. God, however, purposed the universe to be a harmony and not a disharmony, a unity and not disunity. But this can only become a reality when all things and all mankind and all powers in heaven and earth are united in Christ (EPHESIANS 1:9-10). Then all will resound in an awesome celebration of His glory.

What does it mean in the here and now for us to glorify God? It means to worship and adore Him, to honor and praise God extravagantly. Remember the beautiful testimony of Mary after the Angel Gabriel had announced that she was to cradle in her womb the Savior of the world? She sang, *"…My soul glorifies the Lord, and my spirit rejoices in God my Savior"* (LUKE 1: 46-47). Years later when Mary stood at the cross of

Jesus and wept, I believe even in her great agony, her deep sorrow, she continued to celebrate His glory.

Can we do this? When our world tumbles in, when chaos seems to rule the day, when pain and suffering invade our lives—can we still celebrate His glory?

The revelation of the glory of Jesus in our lives is often produced only through pressure and pain, stress and suffering. Are you willing to thank God—not for the suffering and the stress—but for the opportunity it affords you to bring glory to Him? Remember, future rewards will outweigh all our present sufferings (ROMANS 8:18).

Evil will someday wear itself out and come to its logical end—self-destruction. This old earth will pass away, and a New Earth will be born. Then will transpire the glorification of all God's children.

Are you ready to be a participant in the consummation of God's eternal purpose when everything in heaven and earth resounds to His glory? What an awesome celebration this will be!

*"…Worthy is the Lamb, who was slain,
to receive power and wealth
and wisdom and strength
and honor and glory and praise!"*
(REVELATION 5:12)

God's BEAUTIFUL Feet

Two thousand plus years ago Jesus Christ, the God-Man, trod this earth, and He probably did so in flimsy sandals. No doubt His feet often ached as He walked those countless miles. After all, He had no other means of transportation as He went from village to village, city to city, proclaiming the Kingdom of God and performing mercy healings. Perhaps His feet often hurt as sharp pebbles cut into His flesh. For certain, His feet were perpetually dirty and in need of a good scrub. But I know His feet were always beautiful to the Father's eyes, because Jesus was faithfully engaging them in the Cause that counts for eternity.

Never were His feet more beautiful than when He hung on the cross, and they were splattered with blood. Christ was fulfilling His mission on earth. The Lamb without blemish was becoming our atoning sacrifice to reconcile us to the Father.

Before our Lord ascended back to the Father He made this startling statement to His disciples: *"As the Father has sent me, I am sending you"* (JOHN 20:21). Of course, Jesus was not commissioning us to another Calvary. He had fulfilled His redemptive calling; the task was finished. But the Christ was summoning His followers to become God's voice, God's hands, God's "beautiful feet" in this spiritually destitute world. He would no longer be here in a tangible, visible form; but in the personage of the Holy Spirit we could know a mystical union with Christ. Hallelujah!

Paul in his letter to the Roman church talks about the followers of Jesus as having "beautiful feet" when they go as His messengers of peace to a world that is hostile to God (ROMANS 10:15). When one of my international friends who had received Christ during his student years in the States gave his farewell testimony in our church, he said: "O, pray that feet of Choya Tsutsui will be beautiful when he returns to land of Japan." He was simply asking that we pray he would be a winsome witness for the Lord amongst his own people. This young man who once was an alien to God's grace had personally appropriated this verse to his own life.

"O, PRAY THAT FEET OF CHOYA TSUTSUI WILL BE BEAUTIFUL WHEN HE RETURNS TO LAND OF JAPAN."

Take a moment to look at your feet. Mine are not beautiful to gaze upon. But if I dedicate them to the service of my King (despite misshapen toes and protruding bunions), they will be beautiful in His sight. Will you do likewise and heed Christ's invitation to be God's "beautiful feet"?

"Then I heard the voice of the Lord saying, 'Whom shall I send? And who will go for us?' And I said, 'Here am I. Send me!'"
(ISAIAH 6:8)

God's BLESSED Blockades

The Psalmist cried, *"The steps of a good man are ordered by the Lord"* (PSALM 37:23A, KJV). True, indeed! But have you considered this implied truth, "The STOPS of a good man (or woman) are also ordered by the Lord?" The Almighty in His wisdom and love for His children often sends angels or saints (our fellow Christians) to thwart our decisions, to obstruct our paths.

This was certainly the case in Paul's life. He was bent on carrying the gospel to Bithynia in Asia Minor, but for some reason God arrested these plans. *"When they (Paul and his companions) came to the border of Mysia, they tried to enter Bithynia, but the Spirit of Jesus would not allow them to"* (ACTS 16:7). The Apostle was then divinely escorted to Europe, and the gospel spread westward.

Often in my spiritual pilgrimage God has erected barriers that prevented me from making drastic mistakes. He has closed doors but opened promising windows. At the time I was puzzled and on a few occasions even dared to question the Almighty, but then I came to my spiritual senses and acknowledged that His ways are far better than my ways.

On a few occasions I even dared to question the Almighty, but then I came to my spiritual senses and acknowledged that His ways are far better than my ways.

When we pray, we should always ask God to censor our requests. For in earnest dialogue with our Lord we realize we are talking with the One who is All-Wise and All-Loving, and we can trust Him explicitly.

Thank God for intervening in our lives and ordering our "stops" before we make decisions that would shrivel our souls, smudge our characters, or stymie His wonderful dreams for our lives.

^ ST. MAGNUS CATHEDRAL, KIRKWALL, SCOTLAND

"Blessed is the man who listens to me, watching daily at my doors, waiting at my doorway."
(PROVERBS 8:34)

God's Bridge Builders

Jesus Christ has *"freed us from our sins by his blood and has made us to be a kingdom and priests to serve his God and Father..."* (REVELATION 1:5B-6). Peter tells us in one of his epistles that we who belong to Christ are a royal priesthood ordained to declare the praises of Him who called us out of darkness into His wonderful light (1 PETER 2:9).

All Christians are called of God to be priests, to act as intermediaries between people and God. The literal meaning of the word "priest" is "bridge builder". Do you realize that although Jesus is our Great High Priest, we are to be holy and faithful "little priests"? Of course, we cannot absolve anyone of his sins—only Jesus can perform this miracle of grace. However, we can be bridge builders whom the Spirit anoints to lead the lost across the chasm that separates them from the Almighty. Then we can invite them to climb the hill of Calvary where the crucified, risen Savior awaits their unconditional surrender.

> *"MY FRIENDS NEVER ARGUE.*
> *THEY TELL ME MUCH ABOUT JESUS,*
> *AND THEY BUILD THIS BRIDGE OF LOVE*
> *BETWEEN THEIR HEARTS AND MINE.*
> *THEN ONE DAY THIS JESUS 'WALK' ACROSS IT."*

Many years ago on one of our Texas university campuses there was an Oriental student who began attending morning worship at the Baptist Student Center. She was not a Christian, but she was seeking for a peace within that she had never known. Fellow students began to show her the warmth and compassion of Jesus and to share the gospel with her. One day she made the great confession—repented of her sins and trusted Christ for her salvation.

After her baptism some skeptics on the campus approached her and quizzed, "Tell us, what argument did those friends of yours use to convince you to leave your religion and become a Christian?" Some overheard her beautiful response, *"My friends never argue. They tell me much about Jesus, and they build this bridge of love between their hearts and mine. Then one day this Jesus 'walk' across it."*

Simple but profound! We cannot convince anyone of the authenticity of the gospel nor can we convict a person of his sin. This is the Holy Spirit's prerogative. But we can be priests, bridge builders, for the glory of God and the advancement of His Kingdom.

> *BUT WE CAN BE PRIESTS,*
> *BRIDGE BUILDERS,*
> *FOR THE GLORY OF GOD*
> *AND THE ADVANCEMENT OF HIS KINGDOM.*

SUNWAPTA FALLS,
JASPER NATIONAL PARK, CANADA

God's CHANGELESS Character

The Greek gods, like Apollo and Diana, were known for their fickleness. They obviously had moody spells which could cause a flare up of their tempers and an issuing of irrational commands. In fact, they were very much like us—unstable, unreliable, and unsure oftentimes of the proper course of action.

The holy God of the Judeo-Christian faith bears no resemblance to these mythological gods. The prophet Malachi discerns the voice of the Creator as He declares, *"I the Lord do not change"* (MALACHI 3:6A). The Bible assures us that there is no capriciousness in God. *"Jesus Christ is the same yesterday and today and forever"* (HEBREWS 13:8).

The Psalmist tells us that Jehovah God never slumbers (PSALM 121:3-4). He is always alert, attentive to our cries, and available to meet our deepest needs. When we were in Bangkok, Thailand several years ago we saw a mammoth reclining Buddha who was enjoying his afternoon siesta. This idol depicts one who is worshipped by millions even though he never claimed to be divine. Furthermore, his character changed dramatically from the time he was a young man with a wife and child (whom he abandoned) until he became the so-called "Enlightened One" who taught that "All existence is suffering."

◁ *RUINS IN EPHESUS, TURKEY*
Only one lone column remains of the great Temple of Diana, one of the wonders of the ancient world. (Goddess of the moon and of the hunt, called Artemis by the Romans) Reference: ACTS 19:23-41.

The Hindu deities range in the thousands. Krishna, hero of the Bhagavad-Gita (one of the Hindu holy books), is worshipped as an admirable warrior; but he is also a prankster who delights in stealing the saris of the young maidens while they are bathing in a little stream.

The God of the Judeo-Christian faith never vacillates. He is always holy. He is eternally good and wise. He never forfeits His power. Ponder what the Psalmist declared about God: *"In the beginning you laid the foundations of the earth, and the heavens are the work of your hands. They will perish, but you remain; they will all wear out like a garment, like clothing you will change them, and they will be discarded. But you remain the same, and your years will never end"* (PSALM 102:25-27). That is why the only relationship that can be depended upon for a lifetime is our relationship with the great I Am.

THE GOD OF THE JUDEO-CHRISTIAN FAITH NEVER VACILLATES. HE IS ALWAYS HOLY. HE IS ETERNALLY GOOD AND WISE. HE NEVER FORFEITS HIS POWER.

Numerous scriptures tell us that *God's faithfulness endures forever* (PSALM 117:2); *His love and mercy endure forever* (1 CHRONICLES 16:34; JEREMIAH 33:11); *His righteousness endures forever* (PSALM 111:3); *His words and laws endure forever* (PSALM 119:160; 1 PETER 1:24-25).

Join me in praising the God we worship and serve for His enduring, changeless character. He is utterly trustworthy.

God's CONSTANT Care

The big fisherman, who was called the Rock by the Lord Jesus, informed us in his epistle that God cares for us (1 PETER 5:7). Do we tenaciously cling to this assurance—even when our world is caving in? Peter does not give exceptions as to times and seasons when God ceases to care for us. Some folk believe a falling star or an atheist's challenge of His existence may divert His attentions away from us, His "little" children. Such a thought smacks of blasphemy.

The Creator God even notes the tiny sparrow's fall, and He surely never neglects us or turns a deaf ear to our cries. God is everywhere, and the Psalmist tells us that we cannot flee from His presence. Of course, when His children are disobedient they do experience broken fellowship with the Father and a pang of spiritual aloneness. But God still cares, and the Holy Spirit is ever wooing the wayward soul.

Are we convinced that God cares for us when we are suffering physically or emotionally? Often in His wisdom He allows us to know hardships and hazards in order to mature us. Our spiritual growth would be stunted if we were exempt from all life's trials and temptations.

Remember the account of Jesus calming the furious storm on the Sea of Galilee (MARK 4:35FF)? Jesus was sound asleep, but the disciples were terribly frightened. Their little boat was being tossed on the monstrous waves, and they cried out to Jesus, *"Teacher, don't you care if we drown?"* Have you ever uttered a similar cry when the storms of life are battering your soul? The truth is Jesus is in command of all the winds and the waves on the high seas and in our own little lives. And He is still asking, *"Why are you so afraid? Do you have no faith?"*

We may not understand the storms He is allowing to rage in our lives, but we can know with absolute conviction: He constantly cares for us.

Used by Permission of The Great Passion Play, Eureka Springs, Arkansas

"Cast all your anxiety on him because he cares for you." (1 PETER 5:7)

God's COSTLY Salvation

M any years ago when I was involved in International Ministries on the campus of Southern Methodist University, I met Ike, a grad student from India, who was a practicing Sikh. One day Ike burst into my office to exclaim, "Salvation is very cheap in Christian religion. All you have to do to go to Paradise is to say, 'I accept Jesus,' and whoosh! All your sins vanish away forever. Not so in my faith, Eva. Salvation is very difficult. A Sikh must perform many rituals, do good deeds, and read our holy book."

After I had gained my composure and winged a prayer to my Lord, I asked this young alien to God's grace this question, "Ike, has anyone ever taken you up the hill of Calvary?"

With a puzzled look on his face he responded, "No, Eva, I don't think so."

Then I asked permission to do that. With the Spirit's guidance I painted a descriptive verbal picture of Jesus' suffering as the spotless Lamb of God to make possible our salvation. I told him not only of the physical pain of the cross, but of the spiritual agony our Lord experienced on the Tree. But I elaborated that on that day Christ conquered sin and death, and His resurrection three days later validated

all His claims. This is merely a synopsis of what I said to my Sikh friend to help him understand the "naked" gospel—Christianity shorn of its trappings and superficialities. My summary statement I still recall, "Ike, salvation in the Christian faith is offered to the sinner freely; but it was hammered out of the heartbreak and anguish of God."

When I hushed Ike said with a tremor in his voice, "Eva, I have been in this country seven years; but no one ever took me up the hill of Calvary before. Salvation in Christian religion is very costly."

I concluded our conversation that day by explaining to Ike that when someone truly repents and comes to Jesus without personal reservations (confessing Him not only as Savior but as Lord of his life), this can be called an authentic conversion to the Christian faith (ROMANS 10:9-10). Our salvation does not depend upon any spiritual merit we possess but only upon the sacrificial death and triumphant resurrection of Jesus. In the final analysis, I was dependent upon the Holy Spirit to convince Ike of the reality of the gospel and convict him of his self-righteousness. I prayed he would respond to these "wooings" and take this "leap of faith."

Sisters and brothers-in-the-faith, let us never peddle a "cheap grace." And may we never cease to praise Him for His costly sacrifice which made possible our glorious salvation. God gave His one and only Son that we might have eternal life (JOHN 3:16).

Salvation in the Christian faith is offered to the sinner freely, but it was hammered out of the heartbreak and anguish of God.

God's DAILY Deposits

Time is a precious commodity. We have everyone been given the same amount—absolutely no discrimination here. God faithfully deposits daily into our life account 86,400 fleeting seconds, 1,400 precious minutes, and 24 shining hours.

Solomon, in his wiser moments, penned these words: *"There is a time for everything and a season for every activity under heaven"* (ECCLESIASTES 3:1). Then he embellished this declaration. But there are some things, some activities that we need never include on our time agenda. They would be but a terrible waste of the precious moments God has entrusted to us.

We earnestly need to pray for wisdom to set our priorities aright. Remember the day that Jesus was a guest at the home of Martha and Mary? Martha was busy rattling the pots and pans in the kitchen, making last minute preparations for the feast. Mary, however, welcomed Jesus into their Bethany home, and then sat at his feet in rapt attention. Martha was terribly frustrated because Mary had abandoned her. She burst into the parlor and with an unmistakable whine in her voice she asked, *"Lord, don't you care that my sister has left me to do the work by myself?"* Then she had the audacity to issue a command to Jesus, *"Tell her to help me."*

We know the answer the Master gave to Martha. He tried to tell her that worship comes before service. Her timing was all wrong—that was the essence of His seeming rebuke when He said, *"Only one thing is needed. Mary has chosen what is better"* (LUKE 10:38FF).

Paul tells us that we are to make the most of our time, of our opportunities, because the days are evil (EPHESIANS 5:16). This means we daily need divine instruction, the leadership of the Holy Spirit, in order not to abuse this treasure. Fretting instead of "faithing" a bad situation is one way we unnecessarily squander our God-given time. Planning and plotting selfish pursuits is certainly another unsanctified use of the limited tick-tocks we have on planet earth.

Let us begin every dawn with this shout from our hearts, *"This is the day the Lord has made; let us rejoice and be glad in it"* (PSALM 118:24). There is always time to praise God, to delight in His presence, and to declare our allegiance to Him.

One day while I was ministering and witnessing to international students on the Berkeley campus, an Indian friend who had become a devout follower of Jesus, gave me a plaque bearing this inscription: "Only one life 'twill soon be past. Only what's done for Christ will last." This was especially meaningful to me because Chandu, a former Hindu, had believed in reincarnation.

We never know when the death toll will ring for us. When this happens time as we have known it will be no more. Eternity will have been ushered in.

"I will bless the Lord at all times;
His praise shall
continually be in my mouth."
(PSALMS 34:1, KJV)

CHRIST IN THE HOUSE OF MARTHA AND MARY >
By Johannes Vermeer 1655
(National Gallery of Scotland, Edinburgh)

God's DISTURBING Silences

The prophet Habakkuk experienced God's disturbing "silences," but the truth of the matter is: This mouthpiece of the Divine did not realize that the Almighty was working even in the silences. Habakkuk dared to question the Almighty about His seeming indifference to the sin and rebellion of His people (HABAKKUK 1:1-3). God assured him that He was working to remedy the troubling situation. God was sending the Babylonians as His chastening rod to discipline the children of Israel (HABAKKUK 1:6). This news caused the prophet to almost come unglued. Were not the Babylonians even more wicked than the Israelites? Yes, they were—but God can use whomever He pleases to bring His will to pass.

> *HE NEVER VACATES HIS WORLD.*
> *GOD IS ALWAYS AT WORK FULFILLING*
> *HIS SOVEREIGN PURPOSES—EVEN IN THE SILENCES.*

We human beings have to learn that the Father works on His timetable and in ways that we cannot fathom. He never vacates His world. God is always at work fulfilling His sovereign purposes—even in the silences.

Of course, God does not have to explain any of His mighty acts and divine interventions to us. Job realized that eternal verity when the Creator smashed his arrogant complainings with thunderous unanswerable questions (JOB 38:1-41:34).

God just would not be God if we could analyze Him and figure out how He is governing His universe (ISAIAH 55:9). When God does not immediately smash some evil in our world, we are not to question His judgment. This is the divine prerogative; furthermore, God's silences are allowing us human beings to exercise our freedom of choice. Sadly, this often results in chaos and calamity.

> *WHEN GOD DOES NOT IMMEDIATELY*
> *SMASH SOME EVIL IN OUR WORLD,*
> *WE ARE NOT TO QUESTION HIS JUDGMENT.*
> *THIS IS THE DIVINE PREROGATIVE;*
> *FURTHERMORE, GOD'S SILENCES*
> *ARE ALLOWING US HUMAN BEINGS*
> *TO EXERCISE OUR FREEDOM OF CHOICE.*

God is most assuredly working in the silences in your own life. The Almighty One has even given us the perfect formula for healing our mental anguish when we encounter the puzzling enigmas of our day and the seeming silences of Heaven: *"The righteous will live by his faith"* (HABAKKUK 2:4B). You simply must trust Him. He no doubt has bigger plans for you than you could possibly imagine.

What is your Lord doing during all those silences in your life? This must be the answer: *"...He who began a good work in you will carry it on to completion until the day of Christ Jesus"* (PHILIPPIANS 1:6). Rejoice! The Father is silently preparing each of us (His sons and daughters) for the day when we will be glorified.

"Have you ever given orders to the morning,
or shown the dawn its place...?"
(JOB 38:12)

God's ENCOURAGING Ministers

When I speak of "ministers" I am using the term in the broad sense, for every child of God is to be a minister, to be a servant who bears fruit in God's vineyard. This calling is wrapped up in the gift of our salvation.

Some of God's ministers possess the gift of encouragement, a rare quality amongst us humans. Most of us are far too prone to criticize, to discourage, and to point out other's sins and shortcomings. But in your own life, when your courage is lacking, is it not the folk who encourage you who motivate you to stay in the harness for God?

Remember John Mark, the young fellow who was eager to join the missionary team from Antioch (composed of the Apostle Paul and Barnabas, Mark's cousin)? He soon proved to be a grave disappointment to the Apostle. In fact, after Mark's desertion (for reasons unknown to us) Paul dismissed this "quitter" from any considerations as a possible candidate for later missionary ventures. I often wonder if Brother Paul had frightened "the wits" out of the young chap by vividly informing him of the possible dangers lying ahead of them in those "spooky" Taurus Mountains.

PERGA IN PAMPHYLIA, TURKEY
Site where John Mark turned back
(ACTS 13:13)

When the time came for the second missionary journey, John Mark wanted to join the team again. I don't think it was just to "redeem" himself in the eyes of the Apostle, but now he had matured in his faith, and he was eager to serve his Lord in lands where the gospel had never been proclaimed.

Barnabas spoke in Mark's behalf to Brother Paul with the hopes of assuring his teammate that the young fellow was now spiritually equipped for the challenge. But do you recall Paul's response? Adamantly, he refused to grant Barnabas's request. Paul had decided that John Mark just didn't qualify for missionary appointment. But *"Barnabas took Mark and sailed for Cyprus"* (ACTS 15:39B).

John Mark may never have written that first gospel of the life and teachings of Jesus Christ if Barnabas had not believed in his worth as a disciple of our Lord. Barnabas surely lived up to his name, Son of Encouragement. May his tribe increase!

Christ was often engaged in an encouraging ministry. He looked at that impulsive, vacillating, rough fisherman named Simon and called him, *"Peter, the Rock"* (MATTHEW 16:18A). He knew what Simon would become when anointed by the Holy Spirit.

PERHAPS THERE IS A PETER
IN EVERY SIMON WE MEET,
AND IF WE JUST HAD THE EYES OF JESUS
WE COULD SEE HIS DIVINE POTENTIAL.

Perhaps there is a Peter in every Simon we meet, and if we just had the eyes of Jesus we could see his divine potential. Countless others cross our paths from day to day who desperately need a word of encouragement in order to rise above their pitiful, hopeless conditions and discover what they can become when touched by His transforming grace. **Will you be a Barnabas in somebody's life to bring this to pass?**

God's EXHAUSTLESS Riches

Paul, in the queen of his epistles, Ephesians, talks about God's *"unending (boundless, fathomless, incalculable, and exhaustless) riches of Christ {wealth which no human being could have searched out}"* (EPHESIANS 3:8, AMPLIFIED); and, of course, there are many other passages of Scripture that attempt to describe the priceless treasures that are ours as the adopted children of the Heavenly Father.

Why is God pouring these riches into our lives? The key is found in the verse that declares, *"For you know the grace of our Lord Jesus Christ that though he was rich yet for your sakes he became poor, so that you through his poverty might become rich"* (2 CORINTHIANS 8:9). This richness has nothing to do with material gain, an abundance of worldly possessions that are here today and gone tomorrow. No! It is referring to those riches which God has reserved solely for us, His beloved sons and daughters. And they are exhaustless.

THIS RICHNESS HAS NOTHING TO DO WITH MATERIAL GAIN, AN ABUNDANCE OF WORLDLY POSSESSIONS THAT ARE HERE TODAY AND GONE TOMORROW.

The riches begin with His pardon for our sin. Then as redeemed souls we have constant access to the courts of Heaven. Jesus is our Great High Priest who is always available to take our weighty concerns and woeful cries to the Father (HEBREWS 4:14-16). No amount of earthly riches can purchase this astounding privilege because it is only available to those who have been bought by the blood of the Lamb.

Remember the Parable of the Rich Fool? This character was afflicted with a terrible "I" disease and thought he knew the solution to the "problem" of his abundant possessions. He simply had to build bigger and bigger barns in which to store his crops. *"But God said to him, 'You fool! This very night your life will be demanded from you. Then who will get what you have prepared for yourself?' This is how it will be with anyone who stores up things for himself but is not rich toward God"* (LUKE 12:33-34).

Then Jesus said to His disciples who were listening to Him that day, *"Provide purses for yourselves that will not wear out, a treasure in heaven that will not be exhausted, where no thief comes near and no moth destroys. For where your treasure is, there your heart will be also"* (LUKE 12:33-34).

Although the religious leaders during Jesus' time saw wealth as a sign of God's approval, Jesus contradicted such teachings by warning His disciples that worldly riches can actually be a barrier keeping people out of the kingdom of God.

In fact, Christ declared emphatically, *"No one can serve two masters… You cannot serve both God and Money"* (MATTHEW 6:24).

But the paradox of our surrendering all to Jesus is this—we cannot out-give God (LUKE 18:29-30). The riches of grace which He bestows upon His children are indeed exhaustless and unending.

"I built houses for myself and planted vineyards. I made gardens and parks and planted all kinds of fruit trees in them."
(ECCLESIASTES 2:4-5)

"A man may do his work with wisdom, knowledge and skill, and then he must leave all he owns to someone who has not worked for it. This too is meaningless and a great misfortune."
(ECCLESIASTES 2:21)

DUNROBIN CASTLE, SCOTLAND >

God's EXPLICIT Demands

One little phrase can actually summarize God's demands for His children, "Obey me." Religious rituals and sacrifices are never substitutes for subservience to His will and an acknowledgement of His holy commandments. The prophet Amos denounced the temple worshippers who paraded their religiosity but failed to practice God's statues. He bellowed out this word as God's explicit demand they were to heed, *"But let justice roll on like a river, righteousness like a never-failing stream!"* (AMOS 5:24).

And, of course, Jesus simplified what it meant to be one of His disciples with the words: *"Follow me"* (JOHN. 21:19). This invitation, if accepted, is declaring the intention of the receiver to make Christ the Master of his life. Christianity, above all else, is a relationship, an acknowledgment that *"Jesus is Lord"* (ROMANS 10:9-10). This declaration from the depths of one's soul is not optional in the Christian faith. It is an explicit demand.

His demands, however, are never meant to shrivel us but rather to stretch us to our full majestical heights. Half-hearted Christianity always spells human misery. But the devout follower of the Master knows that he cannot out-give God. Of course, He does not give or reward us as the world does. His treasures are not temporal but eternal. Even in this life there are delights for the soul that only the dedicated heart can know.

Psalm 73 tells of a righteous man who was distressed by the seeming prosperity of the wicked, and he dared to question the Almighty about this seeming "injustice." But in his frustration he entered the sanctuary (a place of intimacy with his Lord) and there he realized a tremendous and glorious truth: God was always holding him with His right arm, and he knew a precious fellowship with the Almighty that the wicked never experienced. It was then he cried out with hallelujahs, *"Whom have I in heaven but you? And earth has nothing I desire besides you"* (PSALM 73:25). How could he possibly envy the wicked knowing their loss in the here and now and their fate in the great tomorrow!

HE DOES NOT GIVE OR REWARD US AS THE WORLD DOES.
HIS TREASURES ARE NOT TEMPORAL BUT ETERNAL.
EVEN IN THIS LIFE THERE ARE DELIGHTS FOR THE SOUL
THAT ONLY THE DEDICATED HEART CAN KNOW.

When we are obedient to God, when we desire to follow Jesus in every dimension of our lives, we can expect God's greatest blessing—a deeper, more intimate awareness of His presence in our lives. Accompanying it is a superlative joy as we hear the Father say to us, *"You are my child with whom I am well pleased."*

"This is love for God: to obey his commands.
And his commands are not burdensome."
(1 JOHN 5:3)

God's EXQUISITE *Timing*

According to the inspired Scripture, God brings everything about in His own time. This includes the Second Coming of the Lord Jesus Christ to planet earth (1 TIMOTHY. 6:14-15). The Almighty's timing of every event in human history is impeccable.

The invasion of this earth by the God-Man, Christ Jesus, came *"when the time had fully come"* according to the Apostle Paul (GALATIANS 4:4). God's immaculate timing is revealed in the ripeness of the ancient world for His coming. The very fact that Greek was the universal language greatly contributed to the spreading of the gospel, and the Roman roads facilitated the missionary travels of Paul and his companions. Furthermore, morally and spiritually earthlings were at their lowest ebb. When the world was at its darkest, Jesus

came to be the light of men's shadowy souls.

At this moment God is at work bringing to pass His eternally planned purpose for our lives, and He is always operating on His divine time-table. We often grow impatient and want the Sovereign Ruler of this universe to speed things up, to right all earth's wrongs pronto, and to arrest at once the injustices and insults we are enduring. But the all-wise, all-loving Heavenly Father knows the appropriate time to bring about the restoration of His created order and the consummation of our salvation.

Remember, God is not bound by the restrictions of time and space as we humans are. He knows and sees all that has been, all that is, or ever will be. Our tiny finite minds have difficulty grasping this tremendous truth. The prophet Isaiah heard the voice of Jehovah God declaring, *"As the heavens are higher than the earth, so are my ways higher than your ways and my thoughts than your thoughts"* (ISAIAH 55:9).

Because we know our thoughts and ways are often foolish and faulty, may we joyfully echo David's cry, *"I trust in You, O Lord, I say, 'You are my God.' My times are in your hands'"* (PSALM 31:14-15A).

< THE OLD TOWN
ASTROLOGICAL CLOCK
PRAGUE, CZECH REPUBLIC
Constructed around 1410 A.D.

God's EXTRAORDINARY Resources

The formidable task confronting me at that time was accomplished simply because this one availed herself of His supernatural strength and the wisdom that He always imparts to those who earnestly seek it. In James' epistle he writes, *"If anyone does not know how to meet a particular problem, he has only to ask God and the necessary wisdom will be given"* (JAMES 1:5, PHILLIPS). Of course, we are to believe this promise with all our hearts and shoo away any lingering doubts.

For shame that so often we try to manage life's distresses and dilemmas in our own puny human wisdom and strength. God wants us to be mighty overcomers. For His obedient children, God's boundless resources are always available. We need to cling to this conviction when we are in the misery of a dark valley, a friend's betrayal, a soul-wrenching loss, and when our world is shattered in seemingly unredeemable bits and pieces. Deep within our hearts must reside the staunch belief that God is still on His throne; and His unfailing love will see us through the toughest, most tempestuous moments in our earthly pilgrimage.

Are you availing yourself of His adequate helps—His strength, His sound judgment, His "staying power," His sufficient grace? If so, you can be assured that God will always enable you to meet those extraordinary needs in your life with His extraordinary resources. What a mighty God we serve!

"I (the Lord) will make rivers flow on barren heights,
and springs within the valleys...
I will put in the desert the cedar and the acacia,
the myrtle and the olive...
so that people may see and know,
may consider and understand
that the hand of the Lord has done this..."
(ISAIAH 41:18-20)

Once when I was facing an enormous task and my faith was weakening, God led me to read these words from a source I cannot now recall: *"God will meet extraordinary needs with extraordinary resources."* That day as the Holy Spirit whispered to my heart, I joyfully claimed that promise. Those words reminded me of the Apostle Paul's declaration in one of his epistles, *"I can do all things through Christ who keeps on pouring power into me"* (PHILIPPIANS 4:13). (This is actually a paraphrasing of the verse given by a young preacher lad to a group of black children who were eager to recite the Scripture).

^ *BLACK CANYON OF THE GUNNISON, COLORADO*

God's FITFUL Children

Unlike little Samuel who prayed, *"Speak, Lord, for your servant is listening,"* (I SAMUEL 3:9), are we not often guilty of saying by our attitude if not in literal words, *"Listen, Lord, for your child is speaking?"* It is true we can bring any concern of our hearts to our Heavenly Father, but there are times when we need to practice deliberate stillness and offer up a sacrifice of praise and adoration.

Is there any better way to begin your day than to come reverently into His presence and just sit your soul down and tell it to practice a bit of listening love? Tell your soul to wait in silence before God alone. Then as you and I meditate, we are asking God to give us an undistracted heart, to clean out the cobwebs in our lives, and to give us a fresh vision of His glory.

W hy are God's children so often fitful, restless, and emotionally tied up in knots? Why do we not heed our Lord's voice, *"Be still, and know that I am God"* (PSALM 46:10, KJV)? If we profess to believe that He is sovereign and, therefore, in control of all that is happening in our lives, then how do we account for this self-induced misery?

Perhaps we simply lack stillness and quietness in our lives. The prophet Isaiah counseled, *"In quietness and trust is your strength"* (ISAIAH 30:15). In our daily rush are we allowing the Good Shepherd to lead us beside *"still waters?"* If we are, perhaps we will hear Him say, *"Whatever you need, I Am."*

Perpetual hurriedness can cause us to miss out on many of the blessings God wants to bestow upon us. We must be patient when He asks us to be patient and to wait in expectation for Him to fulfill His promises to us.

We must also learn to be silent in His holy presence.

> ASK GOD TO GIVE US
> AN UNDISTRACTED HEART,
> TO CLEAN OUT THE COBWEBS
> IN OUR LIVES, AND TO GIVE US A
> FRESH VISION OF HIS GLORY.

Surely this is the perfect antidote for the "poisonous" fitfulness that from time to time invades our souls.

*"Speak, Lord,
for your servant is listening."*
(1 SAMUEL 3:9)

God's FLAWLESS Mending

When I was a seminary student, one of my professors, Dr. Jack MacGorman, made this startling statement in class, *"A broken pinion theology is awfully hard on the bird."* My little brain had to wrestle with that profundity. I could just see that poor little robin with its broken wing trying to fly again but then crashing to the ground with an awful thud.

How are we to apply this to us human beings? Sometimes we stumble morally or waver in our faith. When this happens does it mean that we shall never soar again as a disciple of Jesus because we have a broken pinion?

We must not limit our Creator. God, who is omnipotent, can mend our brokenness so perfectly that no fractures in our spiritual pinions will ground us. God who began a good work in us when we were adopted into His family will carry it on to completion until Jesus comes again (PHILIPPIANS 1:6). What an encouragement to human frailty!

> WE MUST NOT LIMIT OUR CREATOR.
> GOD, WHO IS OMNIPOTENT,
> CAN MEND OUR BROKENNESS
> SO PERFECTLY THAT NO FRACTURES
> IN OUR SPIRITUAL PINIONS WILL GROUND US.

Satan, however, wants us to nurse our failures as imperfect children of God. He whispers, *"What makes you think you could ever triumph over your faith collapses, your flirtations with the lust of the eye, your 'yieldings' to the cravings of your flesh?"*

As dearly beloved children of God, we are to denounce the Evil One; for he has no claim on our lives. We know that God who brought us out of darkness into His marvelous light when we were redeemed (I PETER 2:9) will never cease to work miracles of grace in our lives. When we humbly and sincerely ask for forgiveness for the stumblings in our faith and the slippages in our morals, God will mend us so flawlessly that we can soar to even greater heights. What a great and merciful God we serve!

"A broken pinion theology is awfully hard on the bird."

God's "FOOLISH" Message

The unredeemed intellectuals of the world often label those who are devotees of the Christian gospel as foolish and gullible. Rational people (so they contend) simply do not believe in miracles and the supernatural. Those who are aliens to divine grace are often baffled by the confident declarations of faith by the spiritual, the man or woman who has glimpsed the reality of God's glory.

Many years ago my roommate was a brilliant young lady from India, a professing Hindu who never read from one of their holy books or recited any of their religious dogma—except to adamantly proclaim that "all religions of the world are basically the same; the differences are merely peripheral." This, of course, is a common theme of the Hindu faith.

One day Shanta announced to me, "Eva, if there is a God, I shall find Him." I concluded she believed that she could discover the Supreme Being all on her own—just by using her brilliant mind to locate His whereabouts. I was utterly amazed at her assumption.

But, of course, no human being (however brilliant) can accomplish this feat, The Apostle Paul tells us, *"for God in his wisdom saw to it that the world would never find God through human brilliance, and then he stepped in and saved all those who believed his message, which the world calls foolish and silly"* (1 CORINTHIANS 1:21, THE LIVING BIBLE). God has destroyed all human conceived plans of salvation. Instead *"He (God) has chosen a plan despised by the world, counted as nothing at all, and used it to bring down to nothing those the world considers great, so that no one anywhere can ever brag in the presence of God"* (1 CORINTHIANS 1:28-29, THE LIVING BIBLE).

I am reminded of a conversation that the missionary E. Stanley Jones had with Mahatma Gandhi. The setting was an ashram (a spiritual retreat). As they faced the deep question of God, Gandhi said, "The world is a well-ordered machine and we may discover God in obeying its laws, but no miracles are to be expected, and it may take ages." Then he quoted Shankara, a Hindu sage, who said: "He who would find God must have as much patience as the man who would sit on the ocean beach and take up a drop of water on a straw and put it aside and thus empty the ocean by carrying away one drop of water at a time."

As Jones strolled back to his little bungalow he was haunted by those words of Gandhi, "No miracles are to be expected, and it may take ages." And Jones asked himself, "Is that the answer—the best that the highest and noblest living and striving, apart from Christ, can give to the ultimate problems of God and redemption: 'There are no miracles, and it may take ages?'" (<u>Christ at the Round Table</u>).

But then Jones recalled how years ago he had given his "bankrupt soul" to Christ, and a miracle was performed. And it did not take endless ages and countless reincarnations. Since that hour God had become the "supreme reality" in his life. This has likewise been the testimony of countless souls around the world from every tribe and tongue. These transformations, these glorious brushes with the Eternal, resulted not from any human ingenuity but because God revealed Himself to questing souls. The Almighty always takes the initiative; and we human beings respond in submissive faith to His overtures of love and grace.

"This so-called 'foolish' plan of God is far wiser than the wisest plan of the wisest man, and God in his weakness—Christ dying on the cross—is far stronger than any man" (1 CORINTHIANS 1:25, THE LIVING BIBLE).

"For the message of the cross is foolishness to those who are perishing, but to us who are being saved it is the power of God." (1 CORINTHIANS 1:18)

SOLDIER AT THE CROSS BY LARRY COLE >
(Used by Permission of the Artist Larry Cole)

God's FORGIVING Grace

Today as I read the story of David's grievous sins and then his pathetic misery when he realized the love he had trampled under foot, I was reminded of the agony of my soul in days past when I, too, had trifled on God's grace and succumbed to Satan's deceptive nudgings.

But then David, this *"man after God's own heart,"* came to his senses and implored the Holy One of this universe to blot out his transgressions and to restore the joy of his salvation (PSALM 51). And our awesome Heavenly Father reached down and lifted this repentant child into His loving arms.

I, too, have known the incredible love of the great Creator who fashioned me in my Mother's womb. Despite His abundant mercies in my life I, like David, have sometimes brought agony to the Source of all my joy and peace. But, hallelujah, His forgiving grace has cleansed my soul and ushered sweet music back again into my fainting heart.

When we realize how much God has forgiven us when time and time again we have committed sins of the flesh and of the temperament, how can we fail to forgive others who offend us or wound our sensitivities? Jesus told Peter we were to forgive seventy times seven (MATTHEW 18:21-22). Simply stated—we must emulate our Lord and never stop practicing forgiving grace.

If we persist in holding grudges and resentful airs toward others, we better cease praying, *"...forgive us our sins, just as we have forgiven those who have sinned against us"* (MATTHEW 6:12, LIVING BIBLE). Is this not a rather dangerous petition to wing heavenward?

"If you, O Lord, kept a record of sins, O Lord, who could stand? But with you there is forgiveness..."
(PSALM 130:3-4)

< Used by Permission of
The Great Passion Play,
Eureka Springs, Arkansas

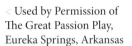

God's "FREE" Gift

Why is it that innumerable companies are incessantly advertising "free" gifts to their prospective buyers? Of course, I realize this is a promotional gimmick that the producers are hoping will entice the receiver to later buy their products. A free sample is supposed to whet our appetite for more of the item being offered as a gift. But isn't a gift supposed to come to us with no strings attached? Why this labeling?

If this is confusing, so are all these tricks of the retailer's trade to my simple way of thinking. A gift should not have to be tagged as a "freebie."

When God offered us the gift of salvation, He did not label it a "free" gift. Of course, it was very costly to God; for it spelled the ignominious death on the cross for His only begotten Son. We read in Ephesians: *"For it is by grace you have been saved, through faith—and this not from yourselves, it is the gift of God—not by works, so that no one can boast"* (EPHESIANS 2:8-9). We do not have to bring our "good" deeds to supplement what Christ has done for us in His atoning sacrifice.

I shall never forget our Afghan friend, Namat, (a devout Muslim) saying, "Eva and Paul, I would like to believe as you do, to have the assurance that when I die I will go immediately into the presence of God. But in my religion I can not know until I face the judgment day whether I have done enough good deeds to offset my bad ones."

We further clarified our convictions by telling Namat that we are saved not by good works but for good works. When we receive this wondrous gift of salvation our hearts are filled with eternal gratitude, and we are eager to become *"God's workmanship created in Christ Jesus to do good works"* (EPHESIANS 2:10).

*WE ARE SAVED NOT **BY** GOOD WORKS BUT **FOR** GOOD WORKS.*

Of course, that gift is only offered to us if we are willing to repent of our sins and all our wrongdoings and accept Jesus Christ as our Savior and Lord. Total allegiance to Him is the divine prerequisite. The gift then is offered only to submissive sinners who are laying all their "idols" on God's altar.

Let us bow our heads this moment and praise God for His awesome gift of salvation, for His redeeming grace.

"For it is by grace you have been saved, through faith—and this not from yourselves, it is the gift of God— not by works, so that no one can boast."
(EPHESIANS 2:8-9)

< *AFGHAN FRIEND VISITING IN OUR HOME IN TEMPLE, TEXAS*

∧ *THE BATTLE OF ISSOS BETWEEN ALEXANDER AND DARIUS—FROM THE RUINS OF POMPEII*

God's FREEDOM Fighter

The greatest battle in all the world was fought on Mount Calvary more than two thousand years ago. The factions of darkness and evil were battling the forces of light and righteousness. The Living Word of God had become flesh to do for us what we could never do for ourselves—overcome the Enemy who plotted the downfall of the human race millennia ago.

As Christians we have unshakeable assurance that Jesus Christ fulfilled His divine mission on earth. He came to liberate us from the entangling chains of sin that long had imprisoned us and alienated us from the Father. The Messiah was appointed as God's freedom fighter; and because of His victory on earth's battleground, we can be set free from our bondage to Satan.

*CHRIST CAME TO SET UP
HIS ETERNAL KINGDOM
OF RIGHTEOUSNESS AND PEACE
IN THE HUMAN HEART.*

When He came to this planet, however, the majority of Yahweh worshippers (Jewish people) misconstrued His battle strategy. They envisioned a political, materialistic Deliverer who would throw off the shackles of the Roman government. In contrast, Christ came to set up His eternal kingdom of righteousness and peace in the human heart.

Even many of the closest followers of Jesus misunderstood the kind of battle He came to wage. Kahlil Gibran, the Lebanese poet, in his book, <u>Jesus: Son of Man</u>, puts these words into the mouth of Judas Iscariot, "Behold, the kingdoms of the world are vast, and behold the cities of David and Solomon shall prevail against the Romans. If thou will be the king of the Jews we shall stand beside you with sword and shield and we shall overcome the alien." "But when Jesus heard this He turned upon Judas, and His face was filled with wrath. And He spoke in a voice terrible as the thunder of the sky and He said, 'Get you behind Me, Satan. Think you that I came down the years to rule an ant-hill for a day?'" Frankly, that is all it would have amounted to—had Christ come only to occupy a Roman throne for a measly day.

But do understand this—the Christ is indeed Lord of Lords and King of Kings; and someday when the God-Man tangibly touches earth again, every knee will bow and every tongue will confess Him as the Sovereign Ruler of all peoples, tribes, and nations (PHILIPPIANS 2:9-11).

WE ARE CALLED TO BE FREEDOM FIGHTERS.

In the meanwhile, we are called to be freedom fighters. Daily we are besieged by enemies—stress, anxiety, weariness of the flesh, or Satanic masqueraders. Our enemies are indeed real, and they are for the most part within ourselves. We desperately need God's help in doing battle against the power of sin. We must not forfeit our freedom in Christ for anything the unredeemed world has to offer.

Although Satan has been fighting a losing battle ever since Calvary, the Evil One is still stomping around on planet earth scouting for captives. Therefore, every sunrise we need to don our spiritual armor (EPHESIANS 6:10-18) and prepare to be freedom fighters under the banner of our Commander-in-Chief, the Lord Jesus.

Paul tells us: *"The weapons we (Christians) fight with are not the weapons of the world..."* (2 CORINTHIANS 10:4). God's mighty weapons are prayer, faith, love, God's Word, and the Holy Spirit.

God's GREEN Meadows

Ours is an age of busyness, of rushing hither and yon. As a result, many people are anxious-hearted and suffer from the effects of constant stress. Surely God does not desire His people to live in a state of perpetual hurry. I believe God wants us to find rest and refreshment for our bodies and our souls. Jesus planned retreats in the mountains for His disciples so that they could get away from the demands of the daily grind and the burdens of their labors.

God's word tells us that we are to *"Be still before the Lord and wait patiently for him"* (PSALM 37:7). Oftentimes we fail to hear the whisperings of the Spirit of God because we are not still enough. We are constantly being distracted by our crowded agendas—the huge list of "things" we think we absolutely must do in any given day.

The famous Shepherd Psalm records these words about David's Lord: *"He lets me rest in green meadows; he leads me*

beside peaceful streams. He renews my strength" (PSALM 23:2-3, NEW LIVING TRANSLATION). Do you want the tension in your body and the weariness of your flesh to be whisked away? Then try resting in those green meadows—that sanctuary God has prepared for you where you can be quiet for a spell, where you can be calmed down, and where your soul can be revitalized.

Christ as man knew what it was to be physically exhausted and emotionally drained. In John's gospel we read that *"Jesus, tired as he was from the journey, sat down by the well"* (JOHN 4:6). But as God He could say, *"Come to me, all you who are weary and burdened, and I will give you rest"* (MATTHEW 11:28).

Countless souls try in vain to find a retreat or an escape from the chaos and clamor of the world with its strain and stress; but they ignore the only One who can provide the rest they desperately need. Surely you, unlike the masses, will heed the Shepherd's voice and avail yourself of His "green meadows."

"He lets me rest in green meadows; He leads me beside peaceful streams. He renews my strength."
(PSALM 23:2-3)

GREEN MEADOWS IN TUSCANY, ITALY

God's GRIEVING Heart

God is Spirit, and we are to worship Him in spirit and in truth (JOHN 4:24); but the Scripture often uses anthropomorphic language (attributes human characteristics to God) to enable us to understand the nature of His being. The Bible even speaks of God's heart being grieved or pained.

In the Book of Genesis we read, *"The Lord was grieved that he had made man on the earth, and his heart was filled with pain"* (GENESIS 6:6). This does not mean that God regretted creating humankind or that God had made a mistake. God was grieved because the people chose sin and death thus forfeiting a relationship with Him.

Sin always breaks God's heart because He loves us. Just as the prophet Hosea's heart was torn because of Gomer's unfaithfulness, likewise God's heart suffers agony because of our rebellion and stubbornness. Our sins today continue to deeply distress God's heart.

As Christians we can grieve the Holy Spirit of God who lives within us and with whom we were *"sealed for the day of redemption"* (EPHESIANS 4:30). We bring sorrow to this One when we fail to be kind and compassionate to one another and to walk as Jesus walked.

The opposite of bringing grief to our Heavenly Father is to be a channel of delight and joy to His heart. We are to be faithful stewards of all He has entrusted to us, and this means above all else we are to be agents of His reconciliation (2 CORINTHIANS 5:19).

Let me illustrate. Is there any joy greater for a young father than when he holds his newborn child in his arms? My dear friend, Lawanda, is a nurse who served as a missionary in Nigeria, West Africa for many years. She told me on one occasion that her heart did somersaults when as a student nurse she assisted for the first time in the bringing of a tiny baby into this world. The delight she witnessed on that father's face when he beheld his child sent her into ecstasies. But then the thought crashed into her soul—"Is this not the joy we give to our Heavenly Father when we have shared the gospel with someone and that soul is born into His family?"

Are we daily bringing gladness rather than grief to the heart of God?

*"Sons are a heritage from the Lord,
children a reward from him."*
(PSALM 127:3)

∧ *PROUD DADDY, DENNIS MCBETH,
holding his newborn son, Roy (our spiritual Grandson)*

God's IMPENETRABLE Fortress

So no matter what life hurls your way, remember you have a place of indescribable stability and saneness to which you can always go. God has provided a special fortress, an impenetrable one, inscribed with your name.

A lthough troubles and temptations often threaten to overwhelm us, the Psalmist declared, *"He (God) is my refuge and my fortress, my God, in whom I trust"* (PSALM 91:2). Martin Luther wrote a great hymn entitled, *"A Mighty Fortress is Our God."* The Lord truly is a bulwark that never fails.

We must turn to God in trust and faith and rejoice that we are always in the palm of His loving hands. Nothing can touch us unless He wills it. Therefore, when we suffer, God must have a divine purpose for allowing this particular agony or heartache to invade our lives.

THE LORD TRULY IS A BULWARK THAT NEVER FAILS.

Even in the midst of stark tragedies and natural disasters that shatter our souls, we must hold tenaciously to the conviction that our God is in control. His love blended with His omniscience may permit these distressing things to happen in our personal lives and in our world for reasons that are beyond our wee minds to grasp.

God does, however, have an impenetrable fortress for all His children. Although it does not shield them from life's catastrophes and personal calamities, it is a refuge from utter hopelessness and despair. It is a place of sweet intimacy with Jesus in which they may know His peace in the midst of their trials and tears.

∧ *WALLS AND TOWERS OF DUBROVNIK, CROATIA, MEDIEVAL CITY*

"O Lord, my strength and my fortress, my refuge in time of distress..."

(JEREMIAH 16:19A)

God's IMPERISHABLE Truth

abundant life, to a life of meaning and purpose, to a life of cherished memories (not sad regrets), and to a life that is gloriously free—unencumbered by the follies and falsehoods of all the modern day emissaries of Beelzebub.

Jeremiah, the weeping prophet, must have trembled as he heard the incriminating voice of God declaring, *"Truth has perished; it has vanished from their lips"* (JEREMIAH 7:28B). The nation called Judah had belittled God's revealed word so long that now she could not discern truth from falsehood. She had lost all understanding of eternal verities and was living in bondage to the deceptions and debaucheries of pagan religions.

But God's truth cannot be vanquished. However, an individual soul or a people may persist in snubbing and silencing God's truth until it is completely smothered out in their lives. When this happens they have no spiritual sensitivity and, therefore, no capacity to detect the lies that the Enemy is constantly trying to sneak into their minds and hearts.

The writer of Proverbs said, *"Truthful lips endure forever; but a lying tongue lasts only a moment"* (PROVERBS 12:19). Such God-honoring lips are ever aware that He is the source of all truth and that His truth is unchanging. Furthermore, God's truth is absolute.

Relativism is the dominant curse of our day—the modifying of God's truths in order to alleviate any attacks of conscience or the frowns of society. This is man's brazen attempt to usurp the role that belongs exclusively to the Almighty. The essence of sin is man's desire to play God for himself.

Jesus said, *"I am the way and the truth and the life…"* (JOHN 14:6). He is unquestionably the way of salvation. But He is also the way to the

∧ *MOSAIC, ST. SOPHIA, ISTANBUL, TURKEY*

Plastered over by the Ottoman Turks when converted to a mosque. Uncovered during the restoration. Building now a museum.

God's IMPLANTED Restlessness

King Solomon, in his wiser days, was inspired to write, *"God has set (planted) eternity in the hearts of men"* (ECCLESIASTES 3:11). Wherever anthropologists, linguists, and missionaries have gone in this topsy-turvy world they have found that man is searching for wholeness, for inner cleansing, for peace, for some kind of touch or communication with the Creator of this universe. Man senses his alienation from God;

he suffers from fragmentation and forlornness—an emptiness in his soul that earth's most extravagant treasures and most exotic pleasures cannot fill.

Saint Augustine once said, "The soul is restless until it rests in Thee, O God." This is surely one of the great curses of our day—restlessness in the human spirit. And man in desperation seeks countless futile ways to find the panacea for this ageless malady.

I shall always remember the day Kodera, a brilliant Japanese student at UC Berkeley, burst into my office to confess to me that he was a lonely, miserable man. And I foolishly responded, "Oh, yes, I know you are terribly homesick for your beautiful Kyoto." Then Kodera with a bit of disgust in his voice said, "Oh, Mariko, (the Japanese name I had been given) I have been a lonely, restless, miserable man all my life." Then it was that the Spirit enlightened my dull senses and led me to say, "Kodera, I know what your problem is. You are homesick for your Heavenly Father." Many discussions followed over a period of several months. One day Kodera yielded to the convicting power of the Holy

∧ *DELPHI, ANCIENT GREEK WORSHIP CENTER | KALI TEMPLE, CALCUTTA, INDIA (Dedicated to Goddess of Destruction and Life)*

^ BUDDHIST TEMPLE, THAILAND | JEWISH WORSHIPPERS AT THE WAILING WALL, JERUSALEM ^

Spirit, and he acknowledged Christ as his Savior and Lord. The turmoil in his soul vanished as, seemingly, he heard the Master say, *"Come to me...and I will give you rest"* (MATTHEW 11:28).

Kodera before his conversion had told me that he believed all religions were ridiculous and anybody who would be a Christian was stupid. One day I had the audacity to say to him, "Kodera, I have discovered that you are a very religious man." He was dumbfounded but finally said, "How can you make such senseless statement?" I replied, "Kodera, science is your sacred cow, and every day you bow at the shrine of the electron microscope." Kodera laughed but then he said, "Mariko, I think you speak the truth."

Man has always been incurably religious. However, there is a vast difference between religion and the gospel. Religion is man's effort to find God by means of his own intellectual endeavors, his devotion to some mythological deity, his strict adherence to a creed, or his sacrifices to appease the supposed wrath of the gods.

As Christians we know that nothing other than a personal encounter with the God who has been revealed to us in Jesus Christ can ostracize the restlessness in our souls and replace it with His redeeming grace.

The greatest sickness of mankind has always been, "Cosmic Nostalgia," homesickness for God.

*BLUE MOSQUE, >
ISTANBUL, TURKEY*

God's IMPOSSIBLE Promises

Again and again in the Bible God makes promises to His people that from the human perspective are absolutely impossible. Remember when God told Abraham that his aged wife Sarah who had always been barren was to have a baby boy (GENESIS 17:17; 18:10)? This was incredible news and totally unbelievable—except to the eyes of faith.

Then when the angel Gabriel announced to a young virgin named Mary that she was to become pregnant, the news astounded her; but she simply responded with the words, *"I am the Lord's servant…May it be to me as you have said"* (LUKE 1:38). And the child she was to birth would be the very Son of God. The fulfillment of that promise to Mary spelled the greatest miracle of all the ages—the Incarnation, the coming of Deity to earth garbed in the frailty of human flesh.

God's promises always seem preposterous and unbelievable to our skeptical world. But with the Almighty "nothing is impossible." However, many earthlings are not candidates for His blessings because they insist they can not "rationally" believe in the supernatural. The Holy Spirit must renew and re-educate their minds (ROMANS 12:2).

The other extreme, however, are those gullible souls who have been misled by the proclaimers of the "prosperity gospel." They have been falsely taught to believe that the Savior promised all who follow Him a primrose path of constant "delights," a life of ease, comfort, and security. On the contrary, Jesus declared to His disciples, *"In this world you will have trouble…"* (JOHN 16:33).

Christians have never been promised health and wealth or an escape hatch from this world's trials and tribulations in exchange for their allegiance to Him. Ah! But we have been assured that despite what life cruelly tosses our way, if we stay in intimate touch with Him we can cope with the "storms" and be *"more than conquerors through him who loved us"*(ROMANS 8:37).

So heed the Master's words and *"Be of good cheer,"* for God is faithful. I confess that despite my spiritual stumblings and my oftentimes anemic faith, my Lord has never abandoned me. He has kept that wonderful promise never to leave me, never to forsake me (DEUTERONOMY 31:6).

As God's obedient child you can claim His promises, perhaps even those the unredeemed world labels "impossible."

"The Lord said to Abram… I will make you into a great nation and I will bless you; I will make your name great and you will be a blessing. I will bless those who bless you, and whoever curses you I will curse; and all peoples on earth will be blessed through you."
(GENESIS 12:1-3)

God's INCOMPREHENSIBLE Mysteries

The Old Covenant is a partial, a fragmentary, revelation of God's attributes and His dealings with the highest of His creation, humankind. Example: God, seemingly, did not superimpose upon Abraham a revelation that was far beyond his day or his understanding. He met this patriarch where he was on his spiritual pilgrimage. God then built upon Abraham's response to this mystery by giving Moses a greater revelation or comprehension of who He was.

CHRIST IS THE LIVING WORD
MADE FLESH.
(JOHN. 1:14)

The story progresses as the Almighty gives the inspired prophets even greater spiritual insights as to His nature and His expectations from His people. The mystery begins to unfold until we come to the fulfillment of Jeremiah's prophecy concerning the New Covenant. This is the consummation, the finale, of God's revelation—never to be superseded. Christ is the Living Word made flesh (JOHN. 1:14).

Someone has defined a biblical mystery as something which was formerly hidden

but has now been unveiled (revealed) in the gospel. Paul's epistles to the Colossians and to the Ephesians speak of this great mystery. Paul declares that as the followers of Jesus we now have the fullness of God's word, the mystery that has been kept hidden for ages and generations, but is now disclosed to the saints. And what are the glorious riches of this mystery? *"Christ in you, the hope of glory"* (COLOSSIANS 1:27B). The "you" embraces all the redeemed—Jew and Gentile alike. C. S. Lewis in his classic, Mere Christianity, says, "There is so much of Him that millions and millions of 'little Christs,' all different, will still be too few to express Him fully."

Of course, without the Holy Spirit's illumination we cannot begin to comprehend this mystery. Our little minds cannot grasp this eternal truth, this profundity, without supernatural intervention.

When we escape the bonds of earth and are promoted to the Father's house, we will have all eternity to explore the awesome mysteries of God and the universe. **How could one possibly think Heaven will be boring?**

"Beyond all question, the mystery of godliness is great: He appeared in a body, was vindicated by the Spirit, was seen by angels, was preached among the nations, was believed on in the world, and was taken up in glory."
(1 TIMOTHY 3:16)

http://www.freejesuschristwallpapers.com/2010/05/jesus-ascension-to-heaven-pictures-and.html

God's INCONCEIVABLE Salvation

With our finite minds we cannot conceive of a God who would stoop so low as to become one of us in order to rescue us from our dilemma of self-love. But the very genius of the Christian faith is that the Creator and Sustainer of this universe lay aside His privileges and priorities as God in order to assume the frailties of human flesh.

Salvation for the crown of God's creation was planned, was conceived, from Eternity. Jesus was the *"Lamb that was slain from the creation of the world"* (REVELATION 13:8). Over the manger of Bethlehem which cradled the Son of God dangled the shadow of a cross. Jesus was born to die—to pay the ransom for the rebellion of the human race.

> *OVER THE MANGER OF BETHLEHEM*
> *WHICH CRADLED THE SON OF GOD*
> *DANGLED THE SHADOW OF A CROSS.*
> *JESUS WAS BORN TO DIE—*
> *TO PAY THE RANSOM*
> *FOR THE REBELLION*
> *OF THE HUMAN RACE.*

Our waywardness and obstinacy, our failure to obey His holy commands, spelled our alienation from His presence. We are undeserving of His mercy and forgiving love. Furthermore, all human efforts to awaken our dead souls have proven futile. God must bring us to life, free us from our chains of egotism, and re-create our shattered souls.

Christianity debunks pride. We must humbly confess our puniness, our nothingness, if we are to avail ourselves of His gift of redemption. If we are willing to perform this simple gesture, the bowing of our knees before Him in authentic sorrow for our misdeeds, He has promised to usher us into His intimacy, release us from bondage to our lower nature, and transform us into new creations in Christ Jesus. We will then be made whole, ready to realize our full potential as adopted children in His perennial care.

Why is it that countless millions resist the wooing of the Holy Spirit, snub the goodness of God, and flee from all that is truly beautiful, soul-satisfying, and eternal? The Enemy persists in twisting the truth, painting a distorted picture of the Christ, and whispering all the while, "There is yet time. God's proposal can wait until you have satisfied the desires of the flesh."

There is tremendous danger in trifling with God's grace. Every time we yield to the Tempter it is easier to become his accomplice.

> *"For to us a child is born,*
> *to us a son is given,*
> *and the government will be*
> *on his shoulders.*
> *And he will be called*
> *Wonderful Counselor,*
> *Mighty God,*
> *Everlasting Father,*
> *Prince of Peace."*
> (ISAIAH 9:6)

MAGGIORE CHURCH >
IN ROME, ITALY

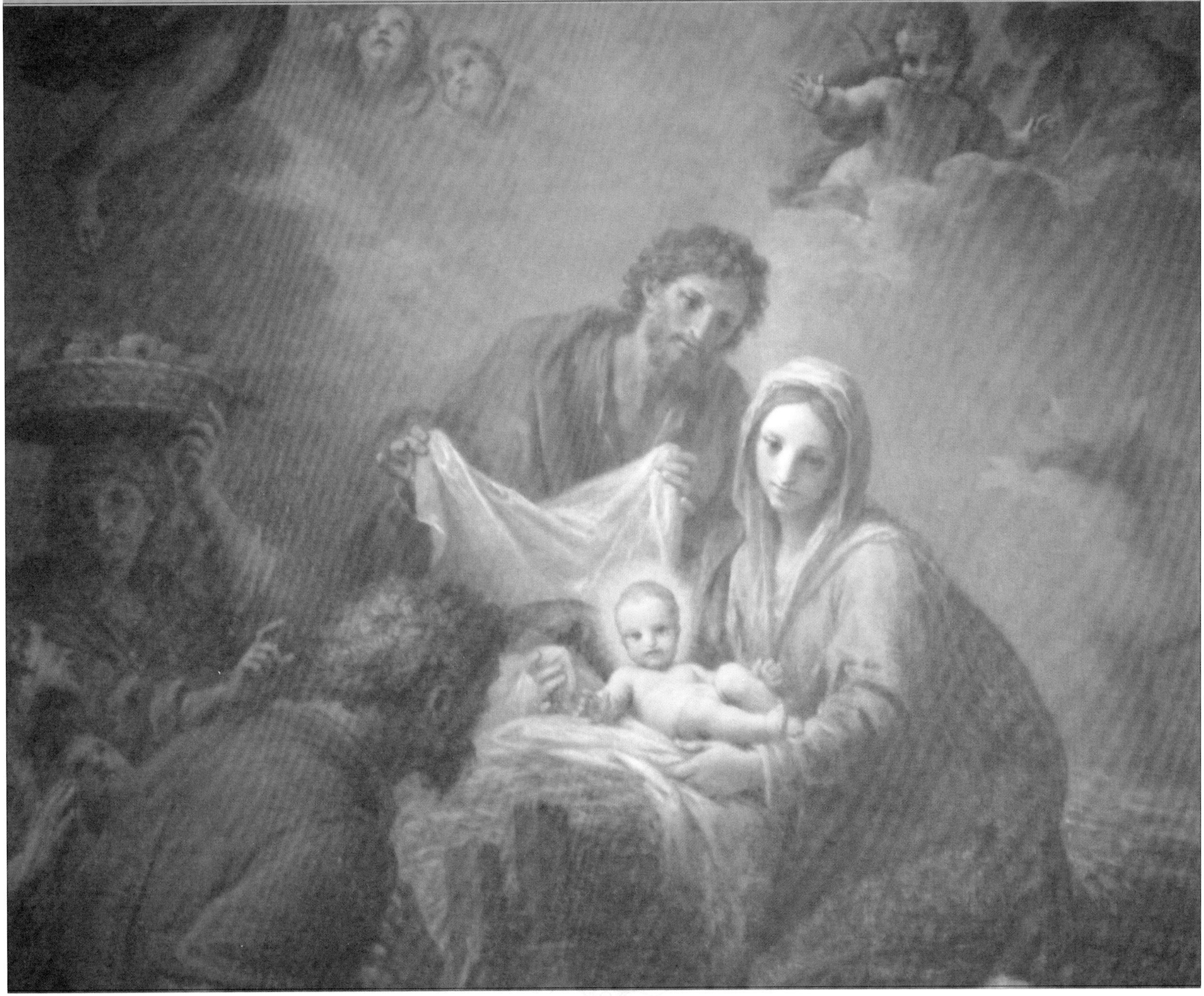

God's INDESCRIBABLE Glory

When believers sing "Glory to His Name", we are voicing our praise and expressing our adoration of God. But how does one describe the glory of God? Certainly it refers to His unique power and greatness, to His majesty and supremacy. Although we cannot see God, from time to time we mortals have been allowed to catch a glimpse of His "glory." The Psalmist sings, *"The heavens declare the glory of God; the skies proclaim the work of his hands"* (PSALM 19:1).

In the Old Testament God's glory is especially seen in the two major events of the Exodus and the Exile. Exodus tells us how the Israelites were led through the desert by the glory of God witnessed in the cloud and in the fire which guided them on their journey. When Moses ascended Mt. Sinai to receive the Ten Commandments, God's glory was manifested. And during the Exile the prophet Ezekiel beheld some amazing visions which unveiled a glimmer of God's glory.

The New Testament declares that Jesus was the glory of God made visible in human flesh. Christ lay aside His privileges and prerogatives as the Lord of the universe and came as a tiny squirming baby to this earth; and the angels in Heaven sang, *"Glory to God in the highest."* The glory of God shines brightest in the face of Jesus Christ. The Apostle John exclaims in his gospel, *"We have seen his glory, the glory of the One and Only, who came from the Father, full of grace and truth"* (JOHN 1:14B).

Those who encountered this Man of Galilee and believed His gospel recognized God's glory in Him.

When Stephen, the first Christian martyr, was giving his bold "argument" to show the validity of the gospel, his persecutors (the Jewish leaders) were gathering stones to hurl at his defenseless body. But Stephen looked above the malice and fury of that Sadducean mob into Heaven, and he saw "the glory of God." He saw the Son of Man *"standing at the right hand of God"* (ACTS 7:56).

A New Testament scholar, G. Campbell Morgan, describes the glory of God in these words: "The most overwhelming testimony of his (Stephen's) death was its witness to the glory of God as being grace." In Stephen's prayer for his murderers there was an echo of the prayer of his Lord when He hung on the cross (LUKE 23:34).

Charles Spurgeon voiced a kindred conviction, "We shall bring our Lord most glory if we get from Him much grace." We glorify God when we "extravagantly" appropriate His grace in our lives and when we continually delight in His presence.

Are you a daily recipient of His grace? If you answered affirmatively to this question, you are indeed a reflection (though in a small measure) of His awesome indescribable glory. *"We, who with unveiled faces all reflect the Lord's glory, are being transformed into his likeness with ever increasing glory, which comes from the Lord, who is the Spirit"* (2 CORINTHIANS 3:18).

"The heavens declare the glory of God; and the firmament sheweth his handiwork."

(PSALM 19:1, KJV)

God's INDESTRUCTIBLE Word

The precious word of God is accessible to countless multitudes today who never even flip through its inspired pages. It is not a charm book designed to ward off danger to those who display it in a prominent place in their houses. However, many a God-breathed passage of Scripture has kept Satan from entering our homes and our lives—when we have used this sword as the Author intended.

God forgive us when we neglect this holy book. Men and women have been persecuted, imprisoned, and even martyred striving to make this manna from Heaven available to a spiritually starving world.

William Tyndale endeavored to translate the New Testament into the English language, but he was tortured and then burned at the stake for his passion to do this. What were his dying words as the flames engulfed his tortured frame? "Lord, open the eyes of the King of England!" Our Lord answered his passionate cry.

In 1611 King James of England appointed Hebrew and Greek scholars in his realm to translate the Bible into the vernacular of the common people. Since that time many devout Bible scholars have given us modern translations that enable us to better interpret God's Holy Word.

However, there are still "peoples" around the world who are deprived of this precious privilege—reading the word of God without fear of being incriminated. Devout followers of Jesus risk their lives this very hour to place this wonderful word of life in the hands of those who are dead in trespasses and sins.

Every day we need to feast on God's word. Often as we pour over the Scriptures we may experience arrows of conviction that pierce our souls. Other times merciful words of consolation and comfort will calm our troubled hearts. Then there are occasions when our minds will be illuminated with spiritual insights, and the wisdom we desperately need to chart our course for a particular day will be given. Whatever resources we need for our earthly pilgrimage God has an adequate supply in His Holy Word.

Read Psalm 119 and praise God for His word spoken through the inspired Jehovah worshippers of the Old Covenant. Saturate your soul with the divine outpourings given to the apostles in the New Covenant. But then shout a glorious hallelujah for the Living Word made flesh in Christ Jesus. This is the consummation of the Father's revelation. It will never be superseded or silenced. God's indestructible word will not return unto Him void but will accomplish what He desires and achieve the purpose for which He sent it (ISAIAH 55: 11).

^ *PRISON IN CARLISLE CASTLE, ENGLAND*

"When he opened the fifth seal, I saw under the altar the souls of those who had been slain because of the word of God and the testimony they had maintained."
(REVELATION 6:9)

RUINS OF THE COLISEUM: DEDICATED IN 82 A.D. BY TITUS >
ROME, ITALY

Many Christians were martyred here because they refused to cry, "Caesar is Lord!"

God's INDISPUTABLE Sovereignty

The God we worship and serve is the Lord of the universe, the King of the cosmos. Nothing happens apart from His Sovereign permissive will—not even the minutest detail. Without the eyes of faith, this is impossible to believe.

Because we live in a fallen world, a Humpty Dumpty civilization, where human beings exercise their freedoms in maddening ways, chaos and corruption abound. The Creator endowed us with this capacity—to glorify Him or to glut our selfish, lustful desires and make an awful mess of everything we touch.

"GOD ALLOWS EVIL MEN AND WOMEN A LOT OF ROPE, BUT REMEMBER THE END OF THE ROPE IS ALWAYS IN GOD'S HANDS; AND HE CAN CALL A HALT ANYTIME HE CHOOSES."

But nothing can thwart God's ultimate purposes. The Sovereign Lord will prevail over every devilish scheme and deceitful shenanigan we earthlings may conjure up (JOB 42:2; PSALM 135:6). I once heard someone say, "God allows evil men and women a lot of rope, but remember the end of the rope is always in God's hands; and He can call a halt anytime He chooses."

God has promised His children a New Earth, one liberated from the Curse. In the meanwhile our Sovereign Lord has assured those who love Him and are called according to His divine purpose (ROMANS 8:28FF) that He can bring unimaginable worth out of all the "nightmarish" occurrences in their lives.

Can you even conceive of a world, a universe, operated by Someone who is not in charge of everything that is happening? If this were so, what hope could we possibly have of a victorious consummation of our faith, a magnificent finale designed to far more than compensate for all our earthly struggles? What hope? None whatsoever!

Rejoice every day in your conviction that nothing can thwart God's eternal purpose for this world and for our lives. His sovereignty is indisputable.

< THE COSMIC BUTTERFLY NASA snapped this image of the planetary nebula, more popularly called the Bug Nebula or the Butterfly Nebula

"The Lord does whatever pleases him, in the heavens and on the earth..."
(PSALM 135:6A)

"THE PILLARS OF CREATION" >
Hubble Space Telescope image of a part of the Eagle Nebula, probably the most famous astronomical image of the 20th Century

∧ *FORUM OF THE MIGHTY ROMAN EMPIRE, ROME, ITALY*

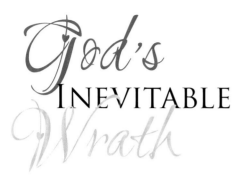

God's
INEVITABLE
Wrath

Some Christians have a difficult time conceiving of the Heavenly Father being angry enough to discipline His children or to chastise them for their waywardness and rebellion. The nation Israel in the Old Covenant was terribly disillusioned when they thought that God would never punish them for their wickedness. They even denounced the prophets who boldly predicted the outpouring of God's wrath and its eminence—due to their violation of the Almighty's revealed will and their persistence in ignoring His warnings.

But, of course, we know that God did allow His chosen people to be taken into captivity and to experience the total destruction of their beloved land. However, God's expression of wrath is always for a divine purpose. In the exile Judah was purged of her idolatry. In Babylon the Potter was molding and shaping Israel into the vessel He desired her to be.

Throughout history great earthly kingdoms (like the Roman Empire) have had their little heyday; but they are destined to crumble if Almighty God is continually snubbed and His laws are ignored. *"The Lord has given full vent to his wrath; he has poured out his fierce anger. He kindled a fire in Zion that consumed her foundations"* (LAMENTATIONS 4:11). America, take heed!

God's anger is not to be identified in any way with our brand of hot headedness and emotional temper tantrums. God is enraged when the crowns of His creation ignore the overtures of His redemptive love and choose a path that leads to the shriveling of their souls. How can the Almighty be indifferent to sin when it always destroys a portion of His image in us?

As Christians God demonstrates His angry displeasure toward us when we deliberately slight His commands and try to hush up His voice within us. The Holy Spirit who dwells in our hearts is grieved, and our "punishment" is that we suffer the loss of His peace and that joy the world cannot take from us. This "emptiness" is designed to lead us to repentance and to the restoration of an intimate fellowship with our Lord.

For those who are rejecting God's grace His wrath upon their pride and self-trust will remain until these souls cry out to Him for mercy and forgiveness.

The Holy Spirit will haunt the rebel, will prick his soul, will woo him to the cross; but in the final analysis God will not coerce him to bow the knee, to give Him his allegiance. If a soul determinedly and conclusively rejects the wondrous love of God, His eternal inevitable wrath is the consequence.

*"Then the word of the Lord came to me,
'O House of Israel, can I not do with you
as this potter does?' declares the Lord.
'Like clay in the hand of the potter
so are you in my hand..."*
(JEREMIAH 18:5-6)

God's INFALLIBLE *Instructions*

The Bible is our infallible instruction book. In its inspired pages we are given specific guidelines as to how to live on planet earth in such a way that we will bring honor and glory to our Creator. In doing so, we will find the greatest meaning and noblest personal fulfillment possible for our own lives.

God has promised, *"I will instruct you and teach you in the way you should go; I will counsel you and watch over you"* (PSALM 32:8). God has individualized instructions for each of our lives; and, as Christians, the Holy Spirit is our teacher who desires to impart this wisdom to us. As we pray we can often hear His voice saying, *"This is the way, walk in it"* (ISAIAH 30:21). But innumerable souls, even some claiming to be children of God, ignore the instruction He wants to give and choose instead to follow the world's untrustworthy "tips" for living a successful life.

After years of pursuing their own selfish ambitions and forfeiting divine instructions, these disillusioned folk achieve what they have been searching for. But now it all turns to ashes in

their mouths and a dull empty ache in their hearts. Success that endures is not measured by what we extract from the world to puff us up for a season or two but how much we invest our lives in our fellow human beings for the glory of God.

Of course, to follow God's instructions may call for one to make sacrifices, to forego the so-called pleasures of this world, to abandon one's own dream castles; but when the last curtain is drawn on the stage of our temporal existence, what will matter for eternity? In capsule form here it is: To hear our Lord say, *"Well done, good and faithful servant… Come and share your master's happiness"* (MATTHEW 25:21)!

Every day God wants to instruct our "goings" and our "comings". He never desires to shrivel us but to stretch us to our full majestic heights as His royal sons and daughters.

Oh, God, help us to listen to Your voice each day and gladly receive Your infallible instructions for our walk and our talk.

< Used by Permission of
The Great Passion Play,
Eureka, Springs, Arkansas

*"This is love for God:
to obey his commands.
And his commands
are not burdensome."*

(1 JOHN 5:3)

"*In all thy ways acknowledge him,
and he shall direct thy paths.*"
(PROVERBS 3:6, KJV)

∧ *AVENUE OF THE GIANTS (Coastal Redwoods, California)*

God's
INNATE
Holiness

"*Holy, holy, holy is the Lord Almighty*" (ISAIAH 6:3)! God's holiness is not acquired; it is innate to His being. Defining holiness is difficult for one to do, for no human being arrives on planet earth with an inborn holiness. In fact, we are tainted with the blemishes of all the Adams and Eves who have gone before us.

God's personhood, in contrast to ours, is altogether pure and untarnished. No evil blotches, no moral lapses, no contaminating impulses are to be found in God's inherent nature.

That, or course, is why the vast chasm exists between the Creator and lowly, sinful humanity. All religions are aware of the vast distance that separates us earthlings from the Holy One. Man in all the great world faiths, except Christianity, is striving to bridge that gulf by his own intellectual and moral endeavors. This is not only difficult; it is impossible.

The Christian gospel declares that God Himself has bridged this awful chasm by the cross of His beloved Son. The sinlessness of Jesus the Christ has become the propitiation for all our wrongdoings. His holiness is imputed to us by our acceptance of His grace, His gift of salvation.

But after this amazing transfer takes place, we are called to emulate our Lord. We are to be holy. Paul tells us in Ephesians *"to put off the old self, which is being corrupted by its deceitful desires…and to put on the new self, created to be like God in true righteousness and holiness"* (EPHESIANS 4:22-24).

◁ GRAND CANYON, ARIZONA

How are we to become holy? The divine intimation is clear to the one who is delighting himself in the Lord. The soul must keep close company with Jesus and allow His goodness and the beauty of His purity to rub off on us.

Actually, according to the prophet Zechariah, there is to be no separation between the sacred and the secular. *"Every pot in Jerusalem and Judah will be holy to the Lord Almighty…"* (ZECHARIAH 14:21). And do we realize that everything we have is to be dedicated on God's altar?

Not just the priest or the preacher is to be holy, but every ordinary child of God is to be an imitation of Jesus. **To our unbelieving world we must be reflections of His glory.**

"Between us (Abraham and the redeemed)
and you (the rich man)
a great chasm has been fixed,
so that those who want to go
from here to you cannot,
nor can anyone cross over
from there to us."
(LUKE 16:26)

God's INTANGIBLE Hands

The Psalmist often praised God because His right hand was shielding him from harm. David was surely rejoicing as he sang those assuring words, *"Though I walk in the midst of trouble, you preserve my life; you stretch out your hand against the anger of my foes; with your right hand you save me. The Lord will fulfill his purpose for me; your love, O Lord, endures forever. Do not abandon the works of your hands"* (PSALM 138:7-8).

But when King David's soul was sorely troubled because he had sinned grievously and had lost the joy of his salvation, he cried out to God, *"... day and night your hand was heavy upon me"* (PSALM 32:4).

Of course, we know that God is Spirit; and they that worship Him must worship in spirit and in truth; so God's hands as described in Scripture are intangible. But the touch of the Almighty is real. And someday those intangible hands will wipe every tear from our eyes (REVELATION 21:4).

These verses and many kindred ones assure me that God is involved in our lives. He is not a distant deity who is indifferent to our human dilemmas. God has even engraved us on the palms of His hands (ISAIAH 49:16).

Other intangibles of God are also mentioned in the Scriptures: His feet, His ears, His eyes. These anthropomorphisms are simply to accommodate our finite minds. Have you never sensed that your Heavenly Father is walking beside you? Have you never felt His everlasting arms helping you to bear your burdens? And never doubt this: His All-seeing eyes are recording in the annals of eternity your every act of mercy, your every testimony of His redeeming grace.

Of course, one day the pre-incarnate Christ did assume the frailties of human flesh. He came down from the splendor of Heaven to literally walk on this sordid earth. His hands reached out to the sorrowful and the suffering. He knew the limitations of man, but He was the exact image of God, His Father. As man He hungered, but as God He fed the 5,000 with a mere five loaves and two fish. As man He thirsted, but as God He offered the living water to satisfy the soul. As man He was often weary; but as God He could say, *"Come unto me all ye who labor and are heavy-ladened, and I will give you rest"* (MATTHEW 11:28 KJV).

God's intangibles are for real. Will you join me in asking the Divine Potter to use His hands to mold us and shape us into the vessel He desires us to be—to the praise of His glory?

"Have Thine own way, Lord.
Thou art the Potter;
I am the clay."

(HYMN, *"HAVE THINE OWN WAY, LORD"*)

∧ Used by Permission of The Great Passion Play, Eureka Springs, Arkansas

God's JUDGMENT Day

Although the Bible tells us that God knows those who are His own (2 TIM. 2:19), the coming of a final Judgment Day is recorded in the Scripture. Matthew's gospel relates to us the last parable that Jesus ever spoke. It is called, "The Parable of the Sheep and the Goats" (MATTHEW 25:31-46).

This story with its spiritual connotation is depicting what will happen when history has been consummated and time is no more. The Lamb of God has won the final battle against all the forces of evil, and Satan's little throne has toppled never to be raised again. All the nations of the world will then be huddled at the feet of the King of Kings.

Christ will separate the sheep from the goats. The sheep, of course, are His followers; but the goats are those who rejected His love and grace.

What is the test on the Judgment Day? How have you loved? Those who had no compassion for the needy, the lonely, and the broken reveal the fact that they have never known the God of love. Those who reached out to human misery wherever they found it validated their faith.

Then the Christ declares to the righteous (those who are wrapped in His spotless robes), *"Come, you who are blessed by my Father; take your*

∧ *FAÇADE OF NOTRE DAME, PARIS, FRANCE*

inheritance, the kingdom prepared for you since the creation of the world. For I was hungry and you gave me something to eat, I was thirsty and you gave me something to drink, I was a stranger and you invited me in, I needed clothes and you clothed me. I was sick and you looked after me. I was in prison and you came to visit me" (MATTHEW 25:36). But then the goats who showed no mercy for suffering humanity are told of their awful fate—an eternal separation from God.

Of course, good deeds are to no avail in the attainment of our salvation. We are redeemed solely by the blood of Jesus, the perfect and ultimate expression of God's grace. But if our faith is authentic, it will be evidenced by our loving concern for others.

"…when the Son of Man comes in his glory and all the angels with him, he will sit on his throne in heavenly glory. All the nations will be gathered before him, and he will separate the people one from another as a shepherd separates the sheep from goats."
(MATTHEW 25:31-32)

*"And the King shall answer ...'
Inasmuch as ye have
done it unto one
of the least of these
my brethren,
ye have done it unto me.'"*
(MATTHEW 25:40, KJV)

HILL COUNTRY, NEPAL

God's LIVING Water

My Nepali Christian friend, Poikail George, joyfully bore "the fellowship of His suffering" when he became a believer. He said to me one day, "The Hindus are like the woman at the well. They are thirsting to know God. But they will not confess it. They venerate their religious tradition. They are very proud people. It is only when you Christians get to know them in a deep, personal relationship that they will confess the emptiness of their religion."

People around the globe are thirsting for truth, for reality, for something or Someone that can satisfy the restlessness in their souls. Some wind up drinking from the filthy cisterns of this world—hoping to find an escape hatch that will give them a bit of calm in their inner being. Others adhere to religious systems that offer potions to satisfy the soul's thirst for spiritual enlightenment. Still a vast majority wrestle with boredom or perennial busyness in the hopes of finding someday a *nirvana* or a more desirable reincarnation.

Jesus declared one day, *"If anyone is thirsty, let him come to me and drink. Whoever believes in me, as the Scripture has said, streams of living water will flow from within him"* (JOHN 7:37-38). The Christ promised abundant life, a God-sanctioned purpose-driven life, to all who drank this water. Such a person might encounter obstacles and ogres around every bend, but his life would still know personal fulfillment and a deep soul satisfaction.

During the days of His flesh, Christ also made a kindred promise to a woman at Jacob's well in the despised land of Samaria. He told her that if she drank this water He was offering her, she would never thirst again. She would find the cure for her meaningless existence, her tormented soul. And she obviously did (JOHN 4:4-30)!

Millions today seek to camouflage their inward discontentment and lack of wholeness. They search hither and yon for a remedy for the malady of their souls. The insatiable pursuit for power, prestige, worldly possessions, or even exotic pleasures never consummates. The answer to this dilemma is a medication that only the Great Physician, Christ Jesus, can dispense—the living water.

THE INSATIABLE PURSUIT FOR POWER,
PRESTIGE, WORLDLY POSSESSIONS,
OR EVEN EXOTIC PLEASURES NEVER CONSUMMATES.
THE ANSWER TO THIS DILEMMA
IS A MEDICATION THAT ONLY THE GREAT PHYSICIAN,
CHRIST JESUS, CAN DISPENSE—THE LIVING WATER.

Of course, as followers of the Master, our thirst for God has not been abetted—it has only been whetted. We want our cups to keep running over with more of His love, His grace, His goodness, His joy, and all the blessings He has in His reservoir for us.

The Apostle John tells us that in the New Jerusalem we will drink eternally from the spring of the water of life (REVELATION 21:6). Hallelujah!

"…If you knew the gift of God and who it is that
asks you for a drink, you would have asked him
and he would have given you living water."
(JOHN 4:10)

^ *HIGHLANDS OF SCOTLAND*

God's LOST Sheep

One day when I was serving as a "foreign missionary on home missions' soil" in Berkeley, California a beautiful Korean girl by the name of Reiko stepped into my office. She asked if I would help her improve her English, especially her understanding of American idioms and our "small talk." I readily agreed, but then I asked her if we could use a modern translation of the Bible as an aid to her learning.

Immediately she responded, "Yes, Bible very good literature; but I do not believe Bible."

"That's all right, Reiko, I replied. "I will teach you anyway."

Then she added with an emphatic tone in her voice, "And I do not believe in the existence of God. Reiko sufficient."

That day I told her this was certainly not true in my life. "Eva not sufficient." I needed God, but I would be glad to assist her any way I could.

The lessons continued for several months. One day Reiko stumbled into my office with her head down, and when she looked up I saw tears trickling down her cheeks. I asked, "Reiko, what is the matter?"

With a trembling voice Reiko blurted out, "Last night Konji and I had big argument." (Konji was her Korean "friend-boy" whom she had met in the States, and she was very fond of him). "I discover that Konji is everything Bible say about man. He is self-centered, egotistical, just like lost sheep he turn to his own way" (ISAIAH 53:6A).

Then trying to control her sobs she murmured, "Eva, is that what's wrong with me, too?"

I replied, "Reiko, my dear, that's what's wrong with Konji, with you, with me, and the whole world. That's why God came in Christ to rescue us from this awful self-love."

That day as we talked and prayed together, Reiko, I believe, caught a vision of Jesus that will accompany her the rest of her days.

NO HUMAN BEING CAN EVER ENTER THE KINGDOM OF HEAVEN UNLESS HE REALIZES HIS LOSTNESS, HIS ESTRANGEMENT FROM GOD.

No human being can ever enter the Kingdom of Heaven unless he realizes his lostness, his estrangement from God. The Good Shepherd who lay down His life for us wants us to confess that we have strayed far away from our Creator. Then He, the Christ, invites us to acknowledge Him as the only one who can deliver us from this self-intoxication and lead us into the Father's loving presence.

"We all, like sheep, have gone astray, each of us has turned to his own way; and the Lord has laid on him the iniquity of us all."
(ISAIAH 53:6)

God's LOVING Denials

Does our loving Heavenly Father always answer our earnest prayers? I believe He always answers the "pray-er," although the specific request of His child may be denied.

Many times our petitions are coated with selfish ambitions and foolish desires that, if granted by the Almighty, would spell disasters for our souls . Be grateful that He said, "No!"

There may be occasions when God has answered "yes" because His people refused to accept His divine revelation and constantly pounded the bars of Heaven with their demands. In Psalms we read that *"He (God) gave them their request but sent leanness into their soul"* (PSALM 106:15 KJV). Frankly, I prefer not to have any shrinkage in my soul; therefore, every sigh and shout I wing to the Holy One must be subjected to His divine approval. If it fails this test, it must be trashed!

"Father, if you are willing, take this cup from me; yet not my will, but yours be done."
(LUKE 22:42)
^ *OH, MY FATHER, by Simon Dewey*

We must emulate Jesus in all our requests to the Father. "Not my will, but Thine be done." Like the Apostle Paul we may discover that the thorns are essential to puncture our pride or our self-trust. Out of our weakness we are made strong in Him—another miracle of God's transformation (2 CORINTHIANS 12:7-10).

Then there are those times in our lives when God seems to say, "My child, the time is not ripe. It is best that I delay the answer to your petition until you have matured in your walk with Jesus. You are still in the kindergarten days of faith. You need to progress from the elementary school of grace to a diligent study of 'the mind of Christ.' Then you will be spiritually ready for that door you have been knocking on to open, for that relationship you have been cultivating to bear fruit, for that dilemma you have been wrestling with to be resolved."

But the Almighty will never tell us to abandon prayer. However, we may learn that we need to invest more time in adoration and praise, more time in stillness before His throne, more time in listening to His whispers of love. And when we delight ourselves in the Lord He will implant within us that for which we ought to desire. It is then that our innermost yearnings come to pass (PSALM 37:4-5).

OUR GREATEST CALLING,
REGARDLESS OF HOW LOWLY OR HOW ESTEEMED WE ARE
IN THE EYES OF MEN, IS TO GLORIFY GOD.

Prayer is, above all else, surrender. This desire to surrender comes from our confident assurance that God is our Heavenly Father who knows what is best for His child and for the Kingdom. Our greatest calling, regardless of how lowly or how esteemed we are in the eyes of men, is to glorify God. Naught else really matters. This is the *summum bonum*!

"Pray continually."
(1 THESSÁLONIANS 5:17)

God's MAGNIFICENT Artistry

∧ *CENTRAL COLORADO*

"He (God) has made everything beautiful in its time..."
(ECCLESIASTES 3:11)

"The heavens declare the Glory of God" shouted the Psalmist (PSALM 19:1). Consider, for example, the puffy clouds that dance across the horizon, the great ball of fire that paints the sky with brilliant hues, the multitudinous stars that pierce the black drapery of night. The list of God's natural wonders goes on and on—every one describing the magnificent artistry of our Creator.

We also see His artistry when a little baby emerges out of the womb, and we know that this is another human being—made in the image of God. Each one is unique. No one is a carbon copy of someone else. Isn't this absolutely mind boggling—the realization that God never duplicates; He always originates?

And He has positioned this world so that we earthlings are in the exact location we should be in reference to the sun. We are in the perfect locale to study and explore the universe. The Master Artist knew precisely where to place our earth when He spoke it into existence. Many renowned astronomers attest to this phenomenon.

Everyday we should delightfully ponder the wonders of God's craftsmanship.

> *EVERYDAY WE SHOULD*
> *DELIGHTFULLY PONDER*
> *THE WONDERS*
> *OF GOD'S CRAFTSMANSHIP.*

Jesus told us to *"Consider the lilies"* (MATTHEW 6:28, KJV). That is, take a few moments each day to appreciate the magnificent artistry of your God. Note the chirping of the bird, the flight of the bumblebee, the sighing of the wind, the shimmering of the aspen leaves, and the lapping of the waves. Paul said, *"...All things are yours,"* (1 CORINTHIANS 3:21) and indeed they are—if we make time to observe and enjoy them as our Lord intended.

May God forgive us for rushing through our days and failing to delight in the wonders of His creation. Let us constantly praise Him for the beauties of the earth that endure despite the often mishandling of these "treasures" by us humans.

BIG SUR, CALIFORNIA

God's MARVELOUS Grace

Ponder with me the marvelous, infinite, matchless grace of God. Someone once defined God's grace as His extravagant goodness. It is something we desperately need, but we do not deserve one whit. The entire human race stands guilty before the One who is holy, the true and living God, who is totally "Other." Man's proud rebellion has spelled alienation from God.

*THE ENTIRE HUMAN RACE
STANDS GUILTY
BEFORE THE ONE WHO IS HOLY,
THE TRUE AND LIVING GOD,
WHO IS TOTALLY "OTHER."
MAN'S PROUD REBELLION
HAS SPELLED ALIENATION FROM GOD.*

But as sinners who have repented and been cleansed by the blood of the Lamb, we shall ever marvel at His grace that is greater than all our sin. But are there not limits to God's forgiveness? Is His marvelous grace to be extended to the vilest and most vicious of creatures?

If you know the story of King Manasseh as recorded in 2 Kings, you will surely acknowledge that Judah never had a more wicked king. He committed every vile, sinful act imaginable—erecting altars to Baal, worshipping the starry heavens, practicing witchcraft, and even sacrificing his own son to a pagan god.

But there is an astounding account of his terrific turnabout recorded in 2 Chronicles. When Manasseh was taken as a prisoner to Babylon, a hook was put into his nose; and he was bound with bronze shackles. The Scripture tells us that *"In his distress he sought the favor of the Lord his God and humbled himself greatly before the God of his fathers. And when he prayed to him, the Lord was moved by his entreaty and listened to his plea…"* (2 CHRONICLES 33:12-13). This atrociously wicked king repented, and God forgave him. Are you stunned at such a revelation of God's grace? Frankly, I am.

Then I began to think of some Manassehs in my own life—people I have "written off" my prayer list, chalked them up as hopeless cases, and decided they have undoubtedly "sinned away their day of grace." But after reading this account, I have asked God to forgive me and to give this one the kind of faith that neither questions the scope nor the limits of God's transforming power and amazing grace.

*MANASSEH,
AN ATROCIOUSLY WICKED KING,
REPENTED AND GOD
FORGAVE HIM.*

Thank God now for His marvelous grace, and go after that Manasseh in your life with renewed hope and divine expectation.

∧ *MILITARY TATTOO, EDINBURGH, SCOTLAND*

Hundreds of bagpipes sounding forth with the hymn,
"Amazing Grace." Awesome!

God's MIGHTY Power

Nothing is impossible to the Omnipotent One. God is all-wise and ever-present. And the staggering truth is: The same power that raised Jesus from the dead is available to us, His followers (EPHESIANS 1:19-20). So what is the problem in our lives? Why do we stumble and stagger so often in our Christian walk?

The answer lies, perhaps, in this factor: The awesome power of our Sovereign God is always available as we face the dilemmas and disasters of life; but this power has not been appropriated in our individual lives.

God will not force His love or His power upon us. We must be willing recipients of His astounding grace and endless supply of spiritual energizing.

Lord God, whatever it takes in my life to make me "more than a

conqueror" in my day-to-day earthly pilgrimage, I pray You will bring it to pass. Those rivers that appear to be uncrossable and those mountains I cannot tunnel through in my own puny human strength are no problem to You, the Omnipotent One. Help me to claim that wonderful promise penned by the Apostle Paul, *"I can do everything through him who gives me strength"* (PHILIPPIANS 4:13). This mighty power we receive from our union with Christ presupposes our commitment to His desire and design for our lives.

Thank you, Master, for revealing Your divine attributes to my questing heart. My earnest longing is to know the mighty power of Your resurrection and to glorify Your name.

< RUGGED DOLOMITES, NORTHERN ITALY

"For since the creation of the world God's invisible qualities—his eternal power and divine nature—have been clearly seen, being understood from what has been made, so that men are without excuse." (ROMANS 1:20)

IGUAZU FALLS, >
ARGENTINA/BRAZIL
(On the Turbulent Parana River)

"Neither this man
nor his parents sinned,"
said Jesus,
"but this happened
so that the
work of God
might be displayed
in his life."
(JOHN 9:3)

"HEALING THE
BLIND MAN" >
Permission given by
the artist Morgan Weistling ©
www.morganweistling.com

God's MIRACULOUS Healings

Mark's gospel is saturated with the wonderful healing miracles of Jesus. The Master even touches a leper, and he is instantly made clean. Christ merely speaks to a mad man, and he immediately gains his sanity. The Great Physician opens blind eyes, unstops deaf ears, straightens the limbs of cripples, and raises the lifeless.

Is God still in the miracle business? Yes! In fact, our doctors may prescribe medications, perform surgeries, and practice psychiatric counseling to alleviate mental and emotional disorders—but God actually does the healing. Christians in the medical profession often make this confession.

> *GOD IS STILL PERFORMING DIVINE SURGERIES—REMOVING SINFUL MALIGNANCIES IN OUR LIVES LIKE PRIDE, JEALOUSY, AN UNFORGIVING SPIRIT, AND COUNTLESS OTHERS. OF COURSE, THE GREATEST OF HIS HEALING MIRACLES IS WHEN A SOUL THAT IS DEAD IN TRESPASSES AND SINS COMES ALIVE IN CHRIST JESUS.*

Sometimes God intervenes in supernatural ways, and an incurable disease is arrested mysteriously. Why God allows others to suffer and their bodies to shrivel, we do not know. However, Joni Erickson Tada is confident she knows why her Lord did not heal her after the accident that left her a paraplegic. She exclaims with a radiant smile words akin to these, "I have an intimacy with Jesus now that I never knew before my 'fortunate' accident."

But there are also abundant miraculous healings of our spiritual illnesses. God is still opening blind spiritual eyes and giving the petitioner 20-20 spiritual vision. God is still touching ears that are deaf to His gentle voice and giving them the capacity to discern His "whisperings." God is still performing divine surgeries—removing sinful malignancies in our lives like pride, jealousy, an unforgiving spirit, and countless others. Of course, the greatest of His healing miracles is when a soul that is dead in trespasses and sins comes alive in Christ Jesus. *"...because of His great love for us, God, who is rich in mercy, made us alive with Christ even when we were dead in transgressions..."* (EPHESIANS 2:4A).

Are you thanking God everyday for the miracles of healing in your own life? If you are spiritually disadvantaged in any way (perhaps a limp in your spiritual walk)—call out to the Great Physician. If you have a spiritual sore that is festering and oozing with sinful poison, ask Him to extract it or smooth His healing balm on it. He is available and eager to make us whole in every dimension of our lives.

God's MOUNTAIN Peaks

That day—etched in our memories forever—we left smoggy Katmandu to hop a small plane that would transport us over the Himalayas. We gasped, and our souls shivered, as we caught our first glimpse of snow-draped Mt. Everest—mystical and magnetic. I almost understood why human beings had risked limbs and lives to climb this perilous peak.

After our awesome spin around this highest mountain range in the world, we returned from "Shangri-La" to attend a Christian worship service in the heart of this Hindu Kingdom. It was a spiritual delight to be in church on the Lord's Day when we were thousands of miles from our homeland.

That morning the pastor read in the Nepali language and then in English this passage of Scripture from PSALM 95: 4: *"In his hand are the depths of the earth, and the mountain peaks belong to him."* When I heard that last phrase I began to sob, for I had stored up within me a tub of hallelujah tears.

I began to think of the many mountain peaks God had given me. This very moment was one of them. Sitting on the floor in this little church with my brown-skinned sisters-in-the-faith

(men sat across the room), we were singing praises to the Living God who had made us one in Christ Jesus.

Through the years my gracious Lord has given me innumerable mountain peaks when I have been amazed at the brilliance of His glory or the bounty of His grace. There have been times aplenty when prayers have been answered enabling me to scale foreboding mountains. There have been countless days when everything has seemed to be in its proper place, moving in the right direction, and coming to a beautiful finale.

But I must not forget the first part of this verse in PSALM 95:4: *"In his hand are the depths of the earth."* At other times I have been in the depths, in the pits of despair or desperation. And life has been hectic even hellish to be honest. But actually when I have realized that His hand was there with me, I have come to know an intimacy with my Lord unknown before.

I humbly confess to you that I have learned more about God when I have been in the pits than I have ever learned about Him while on the mountain peaks. So let us praise God for the "depths" we have struggled in and out of as well as for the mountain peaks we have scaled in our lives.

WORSHIPPERS AT A CHRISTIAN CHURCH
∨ KATHMANDU, NEPAL

We are one in the bond of Calvary love. Our spirits have been joined with the Spirit of God.

"THE ROOF OF THE WORLD:" >
HIMALAYAN RANGE

I humbly confess to you that I have learned
more about God when I have been in the pits
than I have ever learned about Him
while on the mountain peaks.
So let us praise God for the "depths"
we have struggled in and out of
as well as for the mountain peaks
we have scaled in our lives.

God's Nameless Saints

A clarification of the title "saints" may be needed for some people. According to the Scripture, a saint is someone who belongs to Him, our Redeemer and Lord. Remember the Apostle Paul called the church members at Corinth, "saints?" At that time, there were those in this congregation of believers who were engaging in acts or displaying temperaments that were abhorrent to a holy God. And, of course, they had to be reprimanded and called to repentance.

The Bible mentions a few saints whose names are never given to us. One of them was a young slave girl from Israel who was attending the wife of Naaman, a commander of the Syrian army. This valiant soldier was stricken with the dreaded disease of leprosy. One day the little Hebrew lassie told her mistress (Naaman's wife), *"If only my master would see the prophet who is in Samaria! he would cure him of his leprosy"* (2 KINGS 5:3). What remarkable compassion she showed for her master! The God she worshipped had surely taken the bitterness from her heart.

A wonderful miracle of grace then unfolded. Naaman did heed her advice, for he was a desperate man. You will recall how Naaman had to humble himself before Jehovah God before the cleansing could take place. He heeded the simple command of the prophet Elisha, and this foreigner became a devout worshipper of the True and Living God.

Our Lord used this little girl's self-renouncing love to heal and convert her enemy. She is truly one of God's nameless saints.

In the New Testament we have four accounts of the feeding of the 5,000 by the Lord Jesus; but only the Gospel of John informs us that a wee lad was there that day who surrendered his meager lunch to the Master. I can almost see the expression on his little face as he excitedly and gladly handed his five loaves and two fish to the One who fashioned the universe. You know the rest of the story. Thank God for this young boy who withheld nothing from Jesus even though totally unaware of the miracle that was to transpire using his gift. Surely this is another of God's nameless saints.

< ANCIENT MOSAIC IN THE CHURCH LOCATED ON THE TRADITIONAL SITE WHERE JESUS PERFORMED THE MIRACLE OF THE FEEDING OF THE FIVE THOUSAND (JOHN 6:1-15).

The third story of another of God's unnamed saints is mentioned in Paul's personal greetings to the church at Rome. It reads: *"Greet Rufus, chosen in the Lord, and his mother, who has been a mother to me, too"* (ROMANS 16:13). This little phrase is packed with potential meaning for me, for no mention is made in Scripture of any of Paul's biological family becoming followers of Jesus. Perhaps some of them did, but we simply do not know. But much is obvious from this verse: Paul had a Spiritual Mother who must have nurtured him in his faith, encouraged him when he was ridiculed and rejected, comforted him when he grieved over his churches, and met many personal needs in his life. Of this I am assured, the mother of Rufus is one of God's beautiful nameless saints.

Heaven will reward these precious souls. **At this very hour God has His nameless saints who are honoring and glorifying Him in countless inconspicuous ways. You may even be one of them!**

God's NON-NEGOTIABLE *Salvation*

Eternal life is the gift of God's grace. But we are not eligible to receive this gift unless we meet the divine stipulations. They are non-negotiable.

Venkat, my Hindu friend, assured me one day that he had accepted Jesus; but to my dismay I learned that he had merely added Jesus to his pantheon of gods. For after his "confession" he added, "I also worship Rama, Krishna, Ganesh (and he named several other Hindu deities), Buddha, Muhammad, and now your Jesus."

Of course, I had to explain to him that Jesus was not one among many gods. He was the only True and Living God. And no one comes to the Heavenly Father, the great Creator of this universe, except through the Christ. Jesus did not say He was a way, but the way (JOHN 14:6).

God's terms for salvation are non-negotiable. Jesus allowed the rich ruler (LUKE 18:18-30) to walk away from him—still a stranger to God's grace.

Why? This "admirable" fellow who had sincerely attempted to keep the basic commandments of God had, nevertheless, violated the very first decree of the Almighty: *"You shall have no other gods before (alongside) me"* (EXODUS 20:3). This young chap was bowing at the shrine of his vast fortune with no intent of giving Jesus his total allegiance. It has been said, "If He is not Lord of all, He is not Lord at all."

> *"IF HE IS NOT LORD OF ALL,*
> *HE IS NOT LORD AT ALL."*

What is salvation at its core in the Christian faith? It is above all else a relationship. When we come to the cross asking for God's mercy and the gift of eternal life, we must come with no reservations. We burn our idols at His nail-pierced feet and gladly give Him our all.

As we mature in the faith, as the Holy Spirit begins to sanctify us and make us more like Jesus, we will discover additional areas of our lives that need to be surrendered to Him. If we are to be fruit-bearing Christians, faithful disciples, beacon lights for the gospel, we must always listen and obey the counseling and coaxing of the Voice of God that resides within our hearts.

< VENKAT, INDIAN FRIEND,
who has often been in our home to dine
and to discuss spiritual concerns.

God's PEACEMAKING Children

"*Blessed are the peacemakers, for they will be called sons of God*" (Matthew 5:9), so taught the Master on a Galilean mount one day. Note that Jesus did not say "peacekeepers" but rather *"peacemakers."* The latter is a far stronger word, for it is not passive; it calls for action.

Peacemaking is concerned with bringing about a harmonious relationship between "parties" that have been at "odds" with one another. This may be due to unkind or bitter words that have been exchanged or unfortunate misunderstandings that have wounded personal egos. This peacemaking is not an easy task, and we must trust the Spirit of God to give us wisdom, spiritual sensitivity, and compassion.

> *This peacemaking*
> *is not an easy task,*
> *and we must trust the Spirit of God*
> *to give us wisdom,*
> *spiritual sensitivity,*
> *and compassion.*

James in his little epistle says that those who are peacemakers will plant seeds of peace and reap a harvest of righteousness (James 3:18). But the reconciliation may not come about immediately, and we who are striving to be peacemakers may even get caught in the crossfire before the mission is accomplished. I speak from experience.

But what about in our own lives when we know there is someone with whom we have a grievance, and we sense there is a barrier between us? This can even happen between Christian brothers and sisters in the precious *koinonia*. Perhaps an individual has belittled us, ridiculed us, or misjudged us. First, we should examine our own hearts to try to determine what we might have done to provoke such a response. Then we should take the initiative in building a bridge of love to this one who has alienated us. Don't say, "I'll never speak to that person again unless he (or she) apologizes to me." As Christians we must keep forgiving even though this one has spoken ill of us or even shot daggers to our heart. Children of God simply cannot live the abundant life Jesus desires them to know if they harbor resentments or an unforgiving spirit toward any fellow human being. Peacemaking begins on a very personal level.

> *Children of God simply cannot live the abundant life*
> *Jesus desires them to know if they harbor resentments*
> *or an unforgiving spirit toward any fellow human being.*
> *Peacemaking begins on a very personal level.*

Our motivation? Ponder for just a moment the many times you have offended the Lord Jesus either by your indifference to His presence, the utterance of a thoughtless word, or the breaking of a solemn promise. Yet He is always ready to heal the broken relationship and to make peace with His child (Ephesians 2:14-17).

Remember the awful fate of the gingham dog and the calico cat who "side by side on the table sat"? They failed to make peace with one another, had a terrible spat, and ended up devouring one another. Is there a lesson in this for all of God's children?
Compliments of Our Brother-in-the-Faith, >
Christian Cartoonist,
DOUG DILLARD

by Doug Dillard

"Here I am! I stand at the door
and knock.
If anyone hears my voice
and opens the door,
I will come in and
eat with that person,
and they with me."
(REVELATION 3:20)

< *"LIGHT OF THE WORLD"*
By Holman Hunt, Public Domain

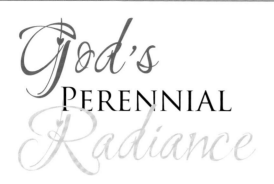

God's PERENNIAL Radiance

The Scripture informs us that *"in him there is no darkness at all"* (1 John 1:5); and I cannot conceive of God without His brilliance, an almost blinding radiance because of His holiness.

David spoke often of God being his light. *"You, O Lord, keep my lamp burning; my God turns my darkness into light"* (Psalm 18:28). In Psalm 36:9 the shepherd king declares, *"...in your light we see light."* Everything is invisible until the light strikes it. We human beings cannot actually see God, but when we sense His loving presence in our lives our darkness vanishes.

> *WE HUMAN BEINGS*
> *CANNOT ACTUALLY SEE GOD,*
> *BUT WHEN WE SENSE*
> *HIS LOVING PRESENCE IN OUR LIVES*
> *OUR DARKNESS VANISHES.*

When Christ, the Living Word, became flesh in the person of Jesus of Nazareth, the gospel writer John announced that *"the true light that gives light to every man was coming into the world"* (John 1:9). But, sad to say, only a precious remnant preferred His light to their darkness. The others chose to walk on in their spiritual midnights because their deeds were evil.

One day when Jesus was in the temple courts He said, *"I am the light of the world. Whoever follows me will never walk in darkness, but will have the light of life"* (John 8:12). But today in far-flung corners of the globe there are followers of the Way who are being cast into dark, damp dungeons—no sunlight from God's heaven invades their cells. However, the testimony of these stalwart souls is that God's light is still with them.

In the Sermon on the Mount Jesus proclaimed these astounding words, *"You are the light of the world...let your light shine before men that they may see your good deeds and praise your Father in heaven"* (Matthew 5:14, 16). So no matter what traumas we are facing in our lives, no matter what fears are hounding our steps, no matter how many tears are coursing down our cheeks, we can still shine brightly for His glory.

When this happens many earthlings (struggling in their spiritual darkness) are amazed as they see His light shining in us despite our trying circumstances. Often this is when they are attracted to our faith, to His glory reflecting in our lives. It is then they may ask us *"to give the reason for the hope"* that we have (I Peter 3:15). Will we be ready and eager at that moment to tell them about our Savior, the Source of our radiance?

*"The Son is
the radiance of God's glory..."*
(Hebrews 1:2)

God's PERFECTLY FITTING Yoke

fitting on you. Keep company with me, and you'll learn to live freely and lightly." (MATTHEW 11:28-30, THE MESSAGE).

When we think about a yoke we envision a heavy wooden harness that fits across the necks of oxen. The animals are then fixed to a piece of equipment (a plow or a wagon) they are supposed to pull. If the yoke does not fit properly, the animal's neck will develop calluses and ugly raw sores.

Sometimes we feel that our world has placed a harsh, sharp, pressing yoke around our shoulders; and we yearn to be released from it. At other times we may be simply carrying a heavy burden, a crushing yoke, of unconfessed sin. Jesus wants to liberate us from all these burdens. An intimate relationship with Jesus can change meaningless, wearisome toil into fruitful productivity.

However, if the Lord is to perform this miracle of grace in our lives, we must heed the commandment of the apostle Paul. *"Do not be yoked together with unbelievers. For what do righteousness and wickedness have in common? Or what fellowship can light have with darkness"* (2 CORINTHIANS 6:14)? Imagine what is likely to happen if a farmer yokes together a short, energetic calf with a tall, sluggish ox—calamity, for certain!

This does not mean we are to shun unbelievers, to have no contact with them. After all, Jesus was the friend of publicans and sinners (LUKE 15:2). But following the wise counsel of the Psalmist, we are not to gather our counsel, our guidance for living, from those who are unredeemed, who delight not in God's law. *"Blessed is the man who does not walk in the counsel of the wicked"* (PSALM 1:1).

So walk with unbelievers but just don't "plow" with them! Because that means—you are harnessing yourself up with those "creatures" whose yokes do not fit. Neither will yours, if you do!

∧ *MALAYSIA, SOUTHEAST ASIA*

Jesus summonsed His disciples to come to Him, and He would ease their burdens and relieve their heavy loads. The Master issued this startling promise, *"Walk with me and work with me—watch how I do it. Learn the unforced rhythms of grace. I won't lay anything heavy or ill-*

Jesus said,
"My yoke is easy
and my burden is light."
(MATTHEW 11:30)

^ *UNIVERSITY OF MARY HARDIN-BAYLOR STUDENTS AT A CHRISTMAS BANQUET,*
FIRST BAPTIST CHURCH, BELTON, TX.

God's PRECIOUS Remnant

As we study world history with the perspective of a Christian worldview, an obvious truth comes to our observation: The faithfulness of the minority eventually triumphs over the might of the majority. That, of course, is presuming that the minority is the recipient of God's love and grace.

*GOD IS COMMITTED
TO PRESERVING A NUCLEUS
OF THOSE WHO ARE OBEDIENT TO HIM.*

Remember the cry of Elijah when he was in the pits of despondency, *"I have been very zealous for the Lord God Almighty. The Israelites have rejected your covenant, broken down your altars, and put your prophets to death with the sword. I am the only one left, and now they are trying to kill me too"* (1 KINGS 19:10). The Apostle Paul reminds us of God's answer to him, *"I have reserved for myself seven thousand who have not bowed the knee to Baal"* (ROMANS 11:4). This was the precious remnant.

Paul continues in his epistle to the Roman Christians, *"So, too, at the present time there is a remnant chosen by grace. And if by grace, then it is no longer by works; if it were, grace would no longer be grace."* (ROMANS 11:5-6). God, in His redemptive mercy, always preserves a remnant. The prophets Isaiah, Jeremiah, and Ezekiel, likewise, proclaimed this glorious truth as they applied it to the people of Israel, God's chosen nation. The Prince of the prophets, Isaiah, explained His plan for a remnant (holy seed) of faithful followers (ISAIAH 6:13B). God is committed to preserving a nucleus of those who are obedient to Him.

Wherever the Dykes have journeyed in God's world they have been made aware that God is always preserving a remnant of believers. Mosques dominate the land of Turkey, and in our travels there we had almost come to the conclusion that no believers inhabited this Muslim nation. Then we took a stroll one afternoon down a busy lane in Istanbul. To our surprise and elation we spotted a little church tucked in one of the alleys. In Nepal, China, and Egypt we had similar experiences. In Israel I was kissed on the cheek by a young Arab teenager who told us he was a Christian and a member of the Baptist Church in Jerusalem.

Praise God for the blessed biblical assurance that He will always preserve a precious remnant. The might of the majority, despite their fierce opposition to Christianity, will never succeed in vanquishing the faithful. A remnant will survive to glorify God.

*"People will come from east and west
and north and south,
and will take their places
at the feast in the kingdom of God."*
(LUKE 13:29)

God's PRE-INCARNATE Appearances

Many examples of these appearances can be cited in the Old Testament—before the Christ became Deity in human flesh. One of the most apparent of these Theophanies (God—appearances) occurred at a burning bush when the Great I Am spoke to a lowly shepherd named Moses. God had a mammoth task for this Hebrew to tackle, and you will recall that Moses supplied the Holy One with several reasons (actually excuses) why he was not the suitable candidate for such a difficult assignment. Eventually he yielded to his Maker, and the Book of Exodus tells us the exciting story of how the Almighty used this meek human being to emancipate the children of Israel from their Egyptian bondage.

But who actually appeared to Moses in the land of Midian that particular day? In John's gospel we read that one day the Master was in the temple when the Pharisees approached him—bent on destroying his powerful grip on the masses. When Jesus bluntly told them, *"Abraham rejoiced to see my day,"* they responded (probably with a smirk on their lips and scorn in their voices). *"You are not even fifty years of age. How can you make such a ridiculous claim?"* And Jesus dropped a bombshell when he said, *"Before Abraham was born, I AM!"* (JOHN. 8:56-58). The Christ is eternal. *"In the beginning was the*

Word, and the Word was with God and the Word was God..." (JOHN 1:1).

Who appeared to Jacob at the Jabbok River? Jacob was wrestling with none other, I believe, than the Christ. And when this notorious schemer finally surrendered to the Lord he became Israel, Prince of God (GENESIS 32:24-30).

One of my favorite "God-appearances" is found in the Book of Daniel. When Shadrach, Meshach, and Abednego were summonsed before King Nebuchadnezzar, they were told that they must bow down and worship his golden image. As devout Yahweh worshippers, they refused to do so. They boldly proclaimed, *"Our God whom we serve is able to deliver us from the burning fiery furnace...but if not...we will not serve thy gods, nor worship the golden image which thou hast set up"* (DANIEL 3: 17-18, KJV). Then they were tossed into the fiery furnace and behold what transpired then! When the king peered into the flames, he saw not just the three Jewish lads walking unharmed but One like unto the Son of Man strolling beside them. This was surely the Christ.

Whenever any human being has had an encounter with the Living God, I believe it has come through the Christ. No man has seen God at any time—so the Scripture informs us. But Christ has manifested Him; Christ has made Him known (JOHN 1:18).

Today there are people around the globe (particularly in Muslim lands) who declare they have experienced in their dreams and visions a personal encounter with the Christ. Are their testimonies bearing evidence of "Post-Incarnate Appearances" of our Savior? If this be so, my heart sings, "Hallelujah!"

< MICHELANGELO'S MOSES
San Pietro in Vincoli, (St. Peter in Chains)
Rome, Italy

God's PRESCRIBED Anti-Depressant

Depression is a common emotional ailment in today's society. Young teenagers who have been bullied by their classmates suffer pangs of despair. Hopelessness often destroys their will to live, and they resort to suicide. Pathetic, indeed!

When we read the Bible (especially the Old Testament) we become aware of the fact that many of God's greatest saints often suffered from despondency and fits of depression. Remember Elijah who was wallowing in his self-pity, informing the Almighty that he was the only loyal worshipper left in the land? This prophet who was a dynamic spokesman for the true and living God had fled the country trembling for his life. Queen Jezebel had frightened the wits out of him.

Then there was Jonah who pouted up a storm because he did not want God to spare those atrociously wicked Ninevites. He must have endured some agonizing days of depression inside the belly of that great sea monster. But when he repented of his obstinacy and called out to his Maker, you remember what happened.

But perhaps the worst case of depression to be found in Scripture belongs to the weeping prophet Jeremiah. He did have a tremendously heart-breaking calling. He was commissioned to tell his people that Jerusalem was going to fall. Even the temple was to be obliterated by the Babylonians. Jeremiah had his days of doubt and despondency, and he even accused God of promising but not delivering (JEREMIAH 15:18B). Jerusalem was still standing and the people of Judah were mocking him. In his dark hours he blurted out some ugly lunatic denunciations—even calling down curses upon the poor man who brought the news to his father, *"A child is born to you—a son"* (JEREMIAH 20:15)!

What was the emotional salvation of these prophets? No matter how far down in the pit they sank they kept talking to God. And God is such an amazingly loving and patient Father that He will listen to our cries—even when they are absurd.

Also, these imperfect heroes of the faith found a way to praise God during their times of grave disappointment and bitter disillusionment. Like the psalmist they rebuked themselves, *"Why are you downcast, O my soul? Why so disturbed within me? Put your hope in God for I will yet praise him, my Savior and my God"* (PSALM 42:5). And Jeremiah in the midst of his sorest trials shouted, *"Sing to the Lord! Give praise to the Lord"* (JEREMIAH 20:13)!

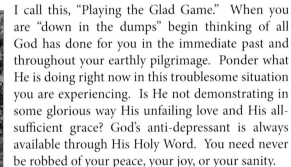

I call this, "Playing the Glad Game." When you are "down in the dumps" begin thinking of all God has done for you in the immediate past and throughout your earthly pilgrimage. Ponder what He is doing right now in this troublesome situation you are experiencing. Is He not demonstrating in some glorious way His unfailing love and His all-sufficient grace? God's anti-depressant is always available through His Holy Word. You need never be robbed of your peace, your joy, or your sanity.

∧ *WAR MEMORIAL IN CANBERRA, AUSTRALIA*

"…They will beat their swords into plowshares and their spears into pruning hooks.
Nation will not take up sword against nation, nor will they train for war anymore."
(ISAIAH 2:4)

God's SOOTHING Consolation

Although Jesus told us that we should never be anxious, who amongst us has not been worried and troubled at crisis times in our lives? When I was scheduled for back surgery some time ago, God brought this verse to my heart's attention during my meditation time: *"When anxiety was great within me, your consolation brought joy to my soul"* (PSALM 94:19). I was totally unaware that this promise from God existed. But there it was—precisely what my disturbed soul needed at that moment.

Then I recalled other occasions when I had experienced God's soothing consolation. It was like a healing balm—this anointing of the Great Physician. The effect was immediate.

IT IS GOOD TO BE ASSURED
HE WILL ALWAYS ANSWER MY PETITION
ACCORDING TO HIS LOVE
AND HIS WISDOM.

God knows our human frailties, and He often rewards our minuscule faith. Remember the man who was distressed because the disciples of Jesus could not heal his epileptic son? Then the man had the audacity to say something akin to this to the Master, *"If you can do anything for my boy, please do it"* (MARK 9:22). Here this human being is asking the Lord of the universe if He can perform a seemingly impossible feat and make his lad whole. And what does Jesus do? He does not reprimand this anxious-hearted father for not recognizing His omnipotence, but with His compassionate heart Jesus reaches out and touches the pitiful child. And he is miraculously healed.

This is truly consolation for my soul. Although my constant cry to God is, "Increase my faith, Lord!" I am grateful that He does not ask for perfect faith when I wing a desperate plea heavenward. It is good to be assured He will always answer my petition according to His love and His wisdom.

Do you need a fresh application of His soothing consolation today? It is available for the sincere asking. Jesus can make the woeful heart sing again.

"Fair are the meadows,

Fairest still the woodlands,

Robed in the blooming

garb of spring;

Jesus is fairer,

Jesus is purer,

Who makes the woeful heart to sing."

(Hymn: "Fairest Lord Jesus")

SPRINGTIME IN TEXAS

God's STAGGERING Proposal

We have been redeemed to be His ambassadors created in Christ Jesus (2 CORINTHIANS 5:20). And He has promised to equip us with all we need to fulfill our royal commission. The Holy Spirit has taken up permanent residence in our hearts to be the instigator of all that transpires as we simply allow Him to "master" us and to speak through us. Although this Third Person of the Trinity must convince aliens to God's grace of the reality of the gospel, convict them of sin, and transport their souls from the land of darkness to the radiance of His glory, the Almighty God has chosen mere humans like us as His personal representatives. We are *"laborers together with God"* (1 CORINTHIANS 3:9, KJV).

The Omnipotent, Omniscient God has proposed to His adopted children a partnership with Him in the task of redeeming the human race. He has chosen flawed and frail humans like us, akin to common clay jars, in which to entrust the most precious treasure in the world—the gospel (2 CORINTHIANS 4:7).

We are ambassadors of the King of Kings and of an Empire that has zero possibility of collapsing because it is eternal. And, wonder of wonders, we are called to play a vital role in the extension of this Kingdom. As His agents of reconciliation, we are to point floundering souls who

are searching for a wholeness and a peace they have never known to a hill called Mount Calvary. In this holy place they are to behold what transpired there some two thousand plus years ago. The Prince of the heavenly Kingdom battled the forces of evil. Christ Jesus conquered sin and death. His resurrection three days later validated all His claims.

The immortal God has chosen us to be His witnesses, to spread the gospel to all the nations. Wrapped up in the same bundle with the gift of salvation we received was the summons to be a spokesman for His Kingdom. We are to use our personal spiritual gifts (whatever they may be) to make disciples. We are God's workmanship created in Christ Jesus to do good works (EPHESIANS 2:10), and the greatest work we can do is to be a faithful proclaimer of the gospel.

God has chosen us with all of our frailties to bear fruit for the glory of His Kingdom. The fruit of a Christian is another Christian. It's the way God planned it.

And He has promised to equip us with all we need to fulfill our royal commission.

*"But we have this treasure
(the incredible good news)
in jars of clay to show that this all-surpassing power
is from God and not from us."*
(2 CORINTHIANS 4:7)

God's STERN Warnings

EACH DAY LET US BE KEENLY AWARE
OF GOD'S WARNINGS
SO THAT WE WILL NOT EXPERIENCE
HIS DISPLEASURE
AND GRIEVE THE HOLY SPIRIT
WHO LIVES WITHIN US.

Jehovah God made many promises to the nation Israel when He entered into covenant with them. They would produce abundant harvests; they would escape the ravages of disease; they would overcome their enemies on the battle fields, etc. They were, after all, God's *"treasured possession"* (EXODUS 19:5).

But their Creator had commanded their obedience as a prerequisite to His blessings. They must forsake all other gods and give Him their total allegiance. If they failed to do this, God would discipline them; He would even allow pagan peoples to devour them. God issued stern warnings to the Chosen Nation. His patience and longsuffering had its limits. His chastisement would be the result of His righteous anger and His unfailing love for these wayward children.

However, the greatest warning the Bible issues again and again to the rebellious human race is simply this: *"He (the Lord) will punish those who do not know God and do not obey the gospel of our Lord Jesus. They will be punished with everlasting destruction and shut out from the presence of the Lord and from the majesty of his power"* (2 THESSALONIANS 1:8-9).

The Holy Spirit is constantly wooing those who are aliens to God's grace. The time may come, however, when the heart is irreparably hardened. When that tragedy occurs the soul has zero spiritual sensitivity, no capacity to respond to the knockings of Jesus on his/her heart (REVELATION 3:20). **God's warnings have been ignored too long.**

Each day let us be keenly aware of God's warnings so that we will not experience His displeasure and grieve the Holy Spirit who lives within us.

Pray to be sensitive to God's chastening rod. Remember, it is Calvary love that is prompting His disciplinary measures. Sometimes He just needs to spank His dear children back into line so that He can embrace them once again.

∧ ST. PAUL'S CHURCH, ROME, ITALY

"...sin is crouching at your door;
it desires to have you, but you must master it."
(GENESIS 4:7)

God's warning to Cain.
And the Holy Spirit often counsels us with a similar warning.

God's SUCCESS Criteria

The world has a distorted concept of what constitutes success. According to most earthlings, the man who is blessed is not the meek but the guy who knows how to get to the "top" in his chosen career or his business venture (no matter what unethical practices have accompanied his "attainments"). He may, however, arrive at his goal only to find that his fame and financial gains have not brought him happiness or a deep inner peace. His heart is still empty, and all his proud achievements have turned to ashes in his mouth and a sickness in his soul. "Meaningless! Meaningless!" (ECCLESIASTES 1:2) All is worthlessness for one who is motivated only by selfish ambition.

A popular notion of success is that it means being able to afford the luxury of hiring others to wash your car, clean your house, or mow your lawn—in other words, to have servants. Jesus said something very contrariwise

to this thinking: "...*whoever wants to become great among you must be your servant*" (MATTHEW 20:26). Success in the Kingdom of God is measured by how many people a person can serve. This concept of success is oblivious to the secular world because servant hood is the very opposite of selfishness.

According to the big fisherman, Simon Peter, "...*God opposes the proud but gives grace to the humble*" (1 PETER 5:5). We are to serve others in humility, for this is the very essence of effective Christian living.

Our perfect example is the Lord Jesus Himself. He left the splendor of Heaven and came to the squalor of this earth not to be served but to serve (MARK 10:45). He was forever extending His love to the lonely, the needy, and the broken.

Is this not what it means to take up our crosses and follow Jesus? We must turn from our selfish ways, toss our egotistical dreams of success onto the dump heap, and allow the Master to live His wonderful life all over again in the ordinary likes of you and me.

Paul exclaimed, "*For to me, to live is Christ*" (PHILIPPIANS 1:21). For us to truly live, to be successful in God's eyes, we must model our lives after His; we must walk as Jesus walked (1 JOHN 2:6). What a tremendous challenge! Frankly, it's impossible!—unless we constantly avail ourselves of the indwelling power of God's Spirit.

< HAPPY CHILDREN WORKING IN A CHRISTIAN ORPHANAGE IN BANGALORE, INDIA

God's SURPRISING Choices

With our finite minds and our inability to foretell the future, we are surprised and even shocked sometimes when we discover that God can use the most unlikely candidates for His eternal purposes. After all, God can choose whomever He pleases. That's His prerogative.

Would you have chosen Jacob, that scoundrel who cheated his brother of his father's blessing and pulled other shenanigans in order to pursue his selfish ambitions? But God knew Jacob's potential if he would but allow the Master Potter to mold and shape him into a fit vessel for the founding of a nation. Jacob would become Israel, the prince of God, and these people would become His "treasured possession." One day (in keeping with the divine timetable) the Son of God would enter the stream of human history. And He would do so through the lineage of Israel. The gospel would then be proclaimed to Jew and Gentile alike.

Of course, there are many others who would never have scored with us as far as prospects for a noble future, a life that glorified the Maker of Heaven and Earth. I am thinking

of that shepherd lad David destined to be the greatest king of Israel and the prototype of the King of Kings, our Lord Jesus Christ. Or what about Jeremiah, the reluctant prophet, who trembled when God whispered his name and called him to a task that demanded a courage he had never known before? Go back even to the great lawgiver, Moses, who was full of excuses when God called him to return to Egypt and lead his people out of bondage. Moses in exasperation finally said, *"O, Lord, please send someone else to do it"* (EXODUS 4:13). But this God would not do.

Why would God choose Jonah to preach to the wicked Ninevites? Why was this reluctant prophet tapped by God to proclaim the JOHN 3:16 of the Old Testament? Frankly, the answer eludes us; but we are confident that God knows precisely what He is doing when He chooses (in our estimation) such unpromising characters.

God's choice of Israel may baffle us because they were an insignificant people, actually a puny people when God called them. But God knew the precious remnant would carry out His ordained purposes for sinful humanity; and the New Covenant, prophesied by Jeremiah, would become a glorious reality (JEREMIAH 31:31-34).

Listen and you may hear, to your surprise, the all-wise, all-loving Heavenly Father, saying, *"You have not chosen Me, but I have chosen you to go and bear fruit—fruit that will last"* (JOHN 15:16). You may be surprised, but I trust you will be elated and eager to respond.

STATUE OF DAVID
BY NICOLAS CORDIER: BASILICA OF
SANTA MARIA MAGGIORE,
ROME, ITALY

God's SWEET *Peace*

One of life's greatest pursuits—common to all humankind—is the desperate search for peace, a peace that endures "come what may." This peace cannot be bought or bargained for in any way. It is the gift of God to those who trust Him implicitly regardless of what is happening in their lives or in this Humpty Dumpty civilization, this fallen world.

However, this peace is not stagnation. It is not the deliverance from earth's struggles and sorrows or from our daily frustrations and fumblings. Rather, it is a mystical inner calm even in the midst of life's annoying dilemmas and abysmal distresses (JOHN 14:27). How can this be? It happens when a soul is clinging to the conviction that a Sovereign God is always in control. And that this One, our loving Heavenly Father, is perfectly able to bring tangible good and eternal worth out of all that is happening within and around us.

Why is it then that we so often chase hither and yon to find this "coveted" stability when it is simply ours for the taking from the Prince of Peace, the Lord Jesus Christ? "O, what needless pain we bear—all because we do not carry everything to God in prayer." (HYMN: "WHAT A FRIEND WE HAVE IN JESUS") Even as He stilled the storm on the Sea of Galilee when His disciples were panicking, our Savior can quiet the tempest in our hearts.

May God grant us the spiritual sanity to claim this sweet peace which is the gift of His love to all His children.

< ST. GILES CATHEDRAL, EDINBURGH, SCOTLAND

I MET GOD IN THE MORNING

I met God in the morning
When my day was at its best,
And His Presence came like sunrise
Like a glory in my breast.

All day long the Presence lingered,
All day long He stayed with me
And we sailed in perfect calmness
O'er a very troubled sea.

Other ships were blown and battered,
Other ships were sore distressed,
But the winds that seemed to drive them
Brought to us a peace and rest.

Then I thought of other mornings,
With a keen remorse of mind,
When I, too, had loosed the moorings
With the Presence left behind.

So I think I know the secret
Learned from many a troubled way,
You must seek Him in the morning
If you want Him through the day.

—RALPH CUSHMAN

God's TERMINABLE Patience

God is amazingly patient and longsuffering with our stubbornness and sinful behavior, but there comes a time when God must discipline His people and demolish the wicked. Although the Bible is plush with beautiful promises from God, there are also passages which spell out curses and God's divine indignation against evildoers (DEUTERONOMY 27:14-26).

> *GOD IS AMAZINGLY PATIENT*
> *AND LONGSUFFERING WITH OUR STUBBORNNESS*
> *AND SINFUL BEHAVIOR,*
> *BUT THERE COMES A TIME*
> *WHEN GOD MUST DISCIPLINE HIS PEOPLE*
> *AND DEMOLISH THE WICKED.*

God does warn us of the consequences of our rebellion and disobedience. *"Be not deceived; God is not mocked; for whatsoever a man soweth, that shall he also reap"* (GALATIANS 6:7, KJV). If we persistently sow discord in our families, our churches, and our communities, we will surely reap havoc in our own lives. We cannot sow scorn and ridicule, judgmental attitudes, and pompous airs without these ugly sins of the disposition failing to boomerang into our own lives.

But God's fiercest warning has to do with the consequences of an individual's being determined to ignore the divine prerogatives and decide each day to do everything according to his own carnal desires, his own ego-centered will. Such a reprobate discovers one tragic day

that God will "give him up" or "give him over" to his own appetites and ambitions (ROMANS 1:24, 26, 28). In this passage of Holy Scripture the Apostle Paul is describing the pitiful state of those souls who have persistently ridiculed God's authority, reviled God's truth, and rejected God's revelation.

> *WE CANNOT SOW SCORN AND RIDICULE,*
> *JUDGMENTAL ATTITUDES, AND POMPOUS AIRS*
> *WITHOUT THESE UGLY SINS OF THE DISPOSITION*
> *FAILING TO BOOMERANG INTO OUR OWN LIVES.*

Frank Sinatra often "bellowed" out the song, "My Way." Although the melody was beautiful, the lyrics were offensive to my ears. The song conveys the message of a proud spirit, one who boasts of going through life and doing everything precisely "my way." Is this not a sad commentary on the twisted thinking and tragic pursuit of multitudinous souls in our wacky world today?

Instead of turning to our own way (ISAIAH 53:6) let us cry passionately, ***"I want God's way to be my way every day."*** If we truly mean those words and strive earnestly to follow through on this resolve, our lives will be saved from madness, misery, and meaninglessness.

"Sowing in the morning, sowing seeds of kindness,

Sowing in the noontide and the dewy eve;

Waiting for the harvest, and the time of reaping,

We shall come rejoicing, bringing in the sheaves."

(HYMN, "BRINGING IN THE SHEAVES")

The lyrics to this American hymn were written by Knowles Shaw in 1874 who was inspired by PSALM 126:6, *"He who goes out weeping, carrying seed to sow, will return with songs of joy, carrying sheaves with him."*

This is an analogy between harvest time in the fields of grain and the spiritual harvest of souls resulting from diligent sowing. Tears may accompany the sowing of the gospel seed, but joy comes to the Christian when he sees the fruit of his labors.

SOWING AND REAPING IN RURAL CHINA

God's THANKLESS Children

As God's redeemed children our hearts are to be constantly singing praises to Him (PSALM 30:12). We are to be ceaselessly thanking God for His enduring love and for the rich blessings He heaps upon us day unto day—even moment unto moment.

Remember the ten lepers who were miraculously healed by Jesus, but only one of them returned to express his gratitude? The Master asked, *"Where are the others?"* (LUKE 17:11-19). Is Christ asking the same question today? *"Where are the others I have blessed? Where are the others I have healed? Where are the others whose prayers I have answered?"*

WE ARE TO BE CEASELESSLY THANKING GOD FOR HIS ENDURING LOVE AND FOR THE RICH BLESSINGS HE HEAPS UPON US DAY UNTO DAY— EVEN MOMENT UNTO MOMENT.

Why do we, God's children, so often fail to thank Him when He performs miracles of grace in our lives, when He conquers the demons in our flesh, when He turns our darkness into light, or when He enables us to scale mammoth walls of opposition? (PSALM 18:28-29). Perhaps we need to spend more time with *"the man after God's own heart,"* (1 SAMUEL 13:14) and harmonize our voices with his in exuberant outbursts of song to our kindred Lord.

The Apostle Paul told the Thessalonian Christians that they were to *"Be joyful always, pray continually, and give thanks in all circumstances,* *for this is the will of God for you in Christ Jesus"* (I THESSALONIANS 5:16). Although we may find it difficult to voice thanks to our Lord for the trials and tumults, the sufferings and sorrows we are experiencing, even in these difficult hours we can express thanks to Jesus for His constant nearness, His unceasing sympathy with our weaknesses (HEBREWS 4:15). And we can praise God knowing that ultimately He can bring a new dimension of goodness to our character because of these stressful scenarios.

Our thanks to God should include not only our gratitude for His daily sustenance, His protective strongholds, and His attentiveness to our cries but our overwhelming appreciation for His very being and all His glorious attributes. This we call adoration—a passionate declaration of our love for Him and a joyous celebration of His awesome splendor and mighty power.

Dear Lord, forgive us for our countless failures to say a simple but sincere "thanks" for all You have done in our lives. Thank You, above all else, for giving to us Your great salvation—so rich and so free. Our gratitude also abounds for Your choosing frail, fault-ridden humans like us to serve as Your ambassadors in this world. Such a sacred privilege and staggering responsibility!

Hallelujah!

GOD'S CHILDREN THANKING AND PRAISING HIM IN BANGALORE, INDIA >

^ *CATTLE GRAZING IN NORMANDY, FRANCE*

God's TOTAL Ownership

In one of his psalms David described the ungodly as people whose lips were always lying or boasting or flattering. They responded by exclaiming, *"We will triumph with our tongues, we own our lips—Who is our master"* (PSALM 12:4)?

This is the very essence of sin—the idea that we human beings have no responsibility to use our lips, our voices, our limbs, our gray matter, and every member of our bodies in ways that would honor and glorify our Creator. Furthermore, as Christians we have been "bought with a price," the blood of Jesus. *"So, whether we live or die, we belong to the Lord"* (ROMANS 14:8B).

And everything in this world belongs to our Creator (PSALM 50:12). God has said, *"...every animal of the forest is mine, and the cattle on a thousand hills"* (PSALM 50:10). This translates: The livestock grazing in those green pastures do not actually belong to that rancher even though they carry his brand. God's ownership has been inscribed on these creatures since "day six" (GENESIS 1:24).

---

*THE HOUSE WE CALL OUR HOME
AND ALL THE TRINKETS AND GADGETS THEREIN
BELONG NOT TO US BUT TO GOD.
THIS REALIZATION SHOULD CRUSH
ALL OUR PRIDE AND, HOPEFULLY, PREVENT US
FROM ALLOWING ANY OF LIFE'S FURNITURE
TO MAKE A FOOL OF US.*

Furthermore, every Christian needs to acknowledge that his/her pocketbook belongs to God. The prophet Haggai reminds us earthlings that God has declared, *"The silver is mine and the gold is mine"* (HAGGAI 2:8).

God has simply entrusted His children with certain tangible "goods," and we are to be trustworthy stewards of all our earthly accumulations. Even the jeans I am wearing today belong to God. The house we call our home and all the trinkets and gadgets therein belong not to us but to God. This realization should crush all our pride and, hopefully, prevent us from allowing any of life's furniture to make a fool of us.

---

*GOD HAS SIMPLY ENTRUSTED HIS CHILDREN
WITH CERTAIN TANGIBLE "GOODS,"
AND WE ARE TO BE TRUSTWORTHY STEWARDS
OF ALL OUR EARTHLY ACCUMULATIONS.*

The words of Abraham Kuyper send spiritual tremors up and down my spine, "There is not one square inch in all the universe, over which Christ is sovereign, that He does not cry, 'This is Mine.'" If we voice a booming "amen" to this declaration by our Lord, we can be liberated from our enslavement to those things we clutch and try to preserve for our selfish pursuits. This surrender will then bring us an inner calm and a passion to glorify God with all He has loaned to us for our temporal benefits.

Are you willing to "let go" of anything that is smothering the person God desires you to be? Get rid of all the excess baggage by acknowledging the rightful possessor of all you call, "Mine." God's total ownership is indisputable.

God's TRANSCENDING *Joy*

The shallow joy the world has to offer cannot transcend our sufferings and our sorrows. Why? This is because the kind of joy the unredeemed world offers is dependent upon temporal "delights," and it can only be realized when life is smooth and uncomplicated. This is totally different from the kind of joy the Apostle Paul talked about when he was in a Roman cell.

When Paul and Silas were imprisoned in Philippi, they must have found this joy that could transcend their despicable conditions. Their bodies were bloodied from the beatings, and their feet were fastened in the stocks. But we read in Acts 16 that they began to sing hymns to God. They were praising God and trusting Him to do in their lives whatever would advance the gospel they had been faithfully proclaiming. And the prisoners were listening—surely with amazement and a curiosity to know from whence came this preposterous joy in the souls of their strange cell mates.

What is the explanation for Paul's and Silas's cheerful spirits in such a dark hour? The radiance of His glory was illuminating their souls. They were filled with the Spirit of the Living God, and they were simply bearing the natural fruit of His indwelling. The fruit of the Spirit is not only love, patience, kindness, self-control, and the like, but also joy (GALATIANS 5:22-23).

This joy is certainly not some phony kind of joy one conjures up when he or she has suffered a great loss, nor is it a frigid apathy when one has experienced the wounds of a friend or the painful banishment of a long-cherished dream. But it is a deep confidence that our Lord Jesus knows just how much we can bear. *"The joy of the Lord"* (NEHEMIAH 8:10) enables us to carry on, to fulfill His divine mission for our lives. God's joy can transcend all our earthly misfortunes and human miseries.

---

*GOD'S JOY
CAN TRANSCEND
ALL OUR EARTHLY MISFORTUNES
AND HUMAN MISERIES.*

Remember, our Heavenly Father is never indifferent to our tears and earthly trials. In fact, the Psalmist tells us that God collects our tears in a bottle (PSALM 56:8, KJV).

Although the traumas and tragedies of life may usher in many a temporary midnight in our souls, for the Christian these "darknesses" are destined to vanish. *"...rejoicing comes in the morning"* (PSALM. 30:5B).

"...You have collected all my tears and preserved them in your bottle! You have recorded every one in your book."
(PSALM 56:8, LIVING BIBLE)

*PHOTOGRAPH OF A
PAINTING IN A LITTLE SHOP,
SOMEWHERE IN EUROPE, >
THAT PAUL (EVA MARIE'S SPOUSE)
COULD NOT REFRAIN FROM TAKING
Painter unidentified*

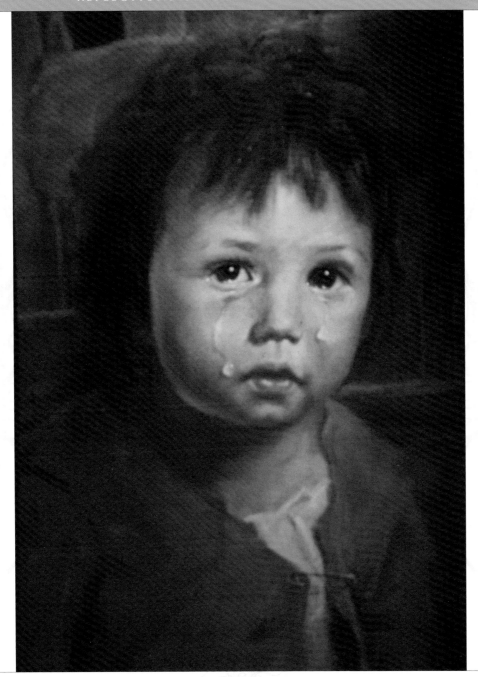

God's UNBREAKABLE Word

Who amongst us has never broken his word, never failed to keep a promise? We have all been guilty of making rash vows which we follow through on with deep regret, or else we trash them with scars on our conscience.

Our Heavenly Father always keeps His word, and He never voices any decree or declamation that is not born of His love and wisdom. He always follows through with His blessing or His displeasure in order to be true to His word. Although man may shun and scorn God's word, he cannot break it. He only breaks himself.

Furthermore, there is no legitimacy for our accepting some of His words but tossing others aside never to be acknowledged. Thomas Jefferson admired the words of the Teacher in the Sermon on the Mount but rejected the miracles of Jesus. The passages about the supernatural healings of Christ were labeled by this "brilliant" man as fictitious, contrary to human reasoning.

But we cannot delete certain portions of Scripture because our little minds cannot grasp them. Nor are we entitled to modify God's word because it offends our sensitivities. My Hindu friends have often said to me, "Eva, Jesus should have said that he was *a* way not **the** way to God—that is too narrow and exclusive." My response has always been, "We, as followers of Jesus, do not question His authority. And if we renounce His word, it imperils our souls."

Psalm 119 is devoted to exclamations about God's word, God's statutes, God's ordinances. We are to hide God's word in our hearts that we might not sin against Him (PSALM 119:11). And He has promised that His word will be a light unto our paths, a lamp unto our feet (PSALM 119:105). Moreover, according to the Apostle Paul, His word is our only offensive weapon, our sword, as we wage battle against the Enemy and his cohorts (EPHESIANS 6:17).

God's word is unchanging; therefore, it is unbreakable. Whatever He has spoken will come to pass according to the divine timetable. For those of us who have become His precious children this is a glorious hope. God is sovereign, and someday this broken, fragmented world will be re-created; and all evil will be vanquished. His word that cannot be broken should be a great treasure-house for our presently earthbound struggling souls.

"Take the helmet of salvation and the sword of the Spirit, which is the word of God."
(EPHESIANS 6:17)

< CHURCH OF ST. PAUL
IN ROME, ITALY

God's UNFAILING

Numerous times the Psalms speak of God's "unfailing love." Although earthly friends may prove untrue and faithless, God's love for His children never wanes. And it is unstoppable—even when we disappoint Him and grieve the Holy Spirit who dwells within our hearts.

Do you realize that *"...the Lord's unfailing love surrounds the one who trusts in him"* (PSALM 32:10)? What a consolation that is to my soul! We should never cease to give thanks to the Lord for His unfailing love (PSALM 107:31). Furthermore, we must strive never to wound this love by our indifference to His presence or our slighting of His commands. *"Love so amazing, so divine, demands my soul, my life, my all."* (HYMN: "WHEN I SURVEY THE WONDROUS CROSS")

I remember Choya, a brilliant Japanese student on the campus of the University of California at Berkeley. In the beginning of our acquaintance Choya announced, "Mariko (Japanese name I had been given), I am very good man. I am much better man than those American students on your campus." Well, I didn't contest that statement because I knew many of those American students to whom he was referring. But as he began to read the Bible I had given him, he began to realize that something vital was missing in his life. One day he burst into my office to exclaim with a tremor in his voice, "Mariko, I am an undone man. I cannot love the way Jesus loved."

This is absolutely true—without the supernatural touch of Jesus upon our lives we self-centered human beings are incapable of loving the Calvary way. This radical, renouncing kind of love can only be ours as we allow Him to be our Lord and to invade every nook and cranny of our lives.

Are you willing to pray, *"Lord, teach me how to love with an abandonment of self?"* *Jesus is no longer here in the flesh—therefore we must allow Him to love this world with all its undesirables through us. This often creates a burning desire in those who see our lives and hear our witness to want to know His redemptive love.*

God's unfailing love will then accompany them as well as us throughout our earthly pilgrimages and into the pearly gates of Heaven.

"This is love; not that we loved God, but that he loved us and sent his Son as an atoning sacrifice for our sins."
(1 JOHN 4:10)

∨ *CHURCH OF THE HOLY CROSS, SEDONA, ARIZONA*

God's UNFATHOMABLE Mercy

What have we done to deserve God's mercy, to merit His tender loving care? Absolutely nothing.

The poet Robert Frost once said, "After Jonah, you could never trust God not to be merciful again." This is the prophet who ran away from God because he did not want to preach to the wicked Ninevites. He feared that if they repented, God would not wipe them off the face of the earth, but in His mercy He would actually forgive them. And this is precisely what did happen. These atrociously evil people cried out to Jehovah, the true and living God, to wipe their dirty slate clean. Amazingly, God forgave Israel's archenemy—much to Jonah's displeasure.

God will teach us how to show mercy— even to the most undeserving and ungrateful. It then becomes a boomerang to our own hearts, "Blessed are the merciful, for they will be shown mercy" (Matthew 5:7). So taught our Lord on a hillside one day.

With the message of this inspired word of God in our hearts, how can we put boundaries on God's mercy and forgiveness? One day more than two thousand years ago Roman justice had decreed the crucifixion of two notorious criminals. That same dark Friday the innocent Lamb of God was to suffer the ignominious death of the cross. Remember, one of the thieves on that occasion had enough spiritual sensitivity left in

his soul that he recognized who Jesus was. He cried out to Him, *"Jesus, remember me, when you come into your kingdom."* And our blessed Redeemer said, *"I tell you the truth, today you will be with me in paradise"* (LUKE 23:42, 43). Mercy triumphed over justice.

We simply cannot fathom God's mercy. But He has commanded us, His ransomed ones, to show mercy to others. Perhaps one of the greatest verses in the Old Testament declares, *"He has showed you, O man, what is good. And what does the Lord require of you? To act justly and to love mercy and to walk humbly with your God"* (MICAH 6:8).

God will teach us how to show mercy—even to the most undeserving and ungrateful. It then becomes a boomerang to our own hearts, *"Blessed are the merciful, for they will be shown mercy"* (MATTHEW 5:7). So taught our Lord on a hillside one day.

"Two robbers were crucified with him, one on his right and one on his left."
(MATTHEW 27:38)

MURAL IN A CHURCH IN EASTERN EUROPE >

God's UNIMAGINABLE *Hereafter*

The prophet Isaiah pictured on the New Earth this idyllic scene when he wrote, *"The wolf will live with the lamb, the leopard will lie down with the goat. The cow will feed with the bear...and the lion will eat straw like the ox* (ISAIAH 116-7).

But, above all else, I am confident that God's unimaginable hereafter will be a glorious place of worship where we all sing and bow in joyful adoration before our blessed Redeemer, the Lamb of God. *"Worthy is the Lamb, who was slain, to receive power and wealth and wisdom and strength and honor and glory and praise"* (REVELATION 5:12)!

God's "tomorrow" for us redeemed sinners is beyond our most extravagant imagination. The Apostle Paul has told us that *"...No eye has seen, no ear has heard, no mind has conceived what God has prepared for those who love him"* (1 CORINTHIANS 2:9). God is not stingy. This, our permanent habitation, will far exceed all our expectations.

The Apostle John, exiled on the Isle of Patmos, had many visions about the bittersweet consummation of history, the bold conquest of the Lamb of God over all demonic powers, and the blissful celebrations when all of the Father's children are gathered to their eternal home.

Whether the streets of the New Jerusalem are literally paved with gold, I do not know. This has never been one of my concerns. I only know that our glorious hereafter will be devoid of all human turmoil and trash. The final chapters of the Book of Revelation describe the perfection of Heaven—no tears, no pain, no death.

Personally, I anticipate something very akin to the Garden of Eden—a place with stately trees, majestic mountains, and trickling streams. I can also imagine the aroma of zillions of roses, gardenias, and other beautiful flowers that are forever budding and blooming to delight our senses! In addition, this one would like an abundance of animals.

The Scripture also informs us that in Heaven, the New Earth, we will be able to sit down at the table with the patriarchs Abraham, Isaac, and Jacob and with believers from every tribe, every tongue (MATTHEW 8:11). The table is the symbol of fellowship, a beautiful kinship of spirit with the saints of all the ages. This, I believe, includes our precious family and friends whose names are written in the Lamb's Book of Life.

God may well have some special assignments for us, but the fulfilling of these duties will spell no weariness, no "worrisomeness" for us but only joy. Perhaps we will explore the cosmos that the Great I Am spoke into existence. Constantly learning! No stagnation! I like the sound of that!

Our sweet moments with Jesus here on "the cursed earth" are just a foretaste of the unimaginable intimacy with Him we shall know someday. He has gone to prepare this perfect habitat for us. No cause, then, for our hearts to tremble when the royal chariot comes to transport us to Glory Land. We are going to a far better place.

^ MASAI MARA GAME PRESERVE, KENYA, EAST AFRICA

DREAM CONCEPT OF THE NEW EARTH >
(Garden of Eden Regained)

"EVE'S" INTERNATIONALS ON THE STEPS OF OUR NATION'S CAPITOL

God's UNIQUE Fatherhood

Islam in its holy book, the Qur'an, speaks often of the power, majesty, holiness, and authoritativeness of Allah, the Muslim word for God. In fact, there are 99 names given to the one that followers of Muhammad worship. However, the father image of God is a concept that is totally alien to the Muslim's belief in the Almighty.

Furthermore, Jesus (Isa in the Qur'an) is no more than a Messenger of Allah. According to Muslim belief, the most blasphemous word that can be uttered is to attribute deity to the Christ. Although Muslims accept the virgin birth of Jesus, they reject the incarnation.

One day I had the privilege of sitting at the feet of the great Wesleyan missionary to India, Dr. E. Stanley Jones. I summonsed my courage to ask him, "Dr. Jones, did Jesus really say He was the only way to God? I have many dear international friends who are devotees of other religions—Muslims, Hindus, Buddhists."

This saint of God then asked me to read the passage from John's gospel where Jesus emphatically said, *"I am the way and the truth and the life. No one comes to the Father except through me"* (JOHN 14:6).

That day Dr. Jones gave me an insight into this Scripture that I shall never forget. He said, "Daughter, it may be possible for your Hindu friend...(And he waited until I said with a quiver in my voice, "Shanta Iyengar.") It may be possible for Shanta to come to Brahman through the disciplines of yoga or through devotion to some mythological deity, but Brahman is not the loving Heavenly Father. Brahman is Impersonal Absolute. There is no concept in Hinduism of God as a loving Heavenly Father Who knows His children by name and Whose concern is measured by a cross."

Our counseling session continued as he said, "It may be possible for your Buddhist friend...(Again he waited until I muttered, "Pompimon.") It may be possible for Pompimon after many reincarnations to experience nirvana (a nebulous state of passionless peace), but this is not the Christian's heaven. There is no concept in Buddhism of God as a loving Heavenly Father Who knows His children by name and Whose concern is measured by a cross."

Dr. Jones concluded our interview that day by declaring, "It may be possible for your Muslim friend...(And once again I stammered a name, "Azar Pedarsani.") It may be possible for Azar to come to Allah through a faithful observance of the Five Pillars of Islam, but Allah is a Heavenly Sultan with an inscrutable will. There is no concept in Islam of God as a loving Heavenly Father Who knows His children by name and Whose concern is measured by a cross."

> *EVEN IF THE DEVOTEES TO THESE OTHER FAITHS LIVED UP TO ALL THE DEMANDS OF THEIR RELIGION, THEY STILL HAVE NO HOPE OF REDEMPTION, NO POSSIBILITY OF KNOWING A PERSONAL RELATIONSHIP WITH GOD AS THEIR LOVING HEAVENLY FATHER.*

Do you grasp the profundity of what Dr. Jones was saying to me that balmy afternoon in Berkeley, California when I sat enraptured in his presence? Even if the devotees to these other faiths lived up to all the demands of their religion, they still have no hope of redemption, no possibility of knowing a personal relationship with God as their loving Heavenly Father.

This is the reason we must heed the Great Commission and be witnesses to all "peoples" beginning with the world on our doorstep.

God's VISIBLE Image

The Apostle John tells us in his gospel that *"No one has ever seen God, but God the One and Only, who is at the Father's side, has made him known"* (JOHN 1:18). This is the consummation of God's revelation which we call the incarnation. Paul clarifies this in Philippians by saying that when Christ left the splendors of Heaven to come to the sordidness of this earth, He assumed the frailty of human flesh. He was the God-Man, fully God and fully man. An inscrutable mystery—yes!

MUSLIM FRIEND FROM PAKISTAN

>

"Anyone who has seen me has seen the Father."
(JOHN 14:9B)

"I and the Father are One."
(JOHN 10:30)

"God was pleased to have all his fullness dwell in him."
(COLOSSIANS 1:19)

One day when I was serving as the Baptist Student Minister and Bible Teacher at Texas Woman's University, a Muslim student burst into my office to exclaim, "You Christians are polytheists. You worship three gods: Mary, mother; Jesus, Son; and God, Father. We Muslims are the true monotheists. We worship one God, Allah; and Muhammad is his prophet."

I tried to explain to her that we, too, were monotheists. We worshipped one God, one Reality; but three expressions or manifestations of the Trinity: God the Father, God the Son, and God the Holy Spirit.

Before I could elaborate she interrupted and said, "And you believe blasphemous thing. You take this Jesus, mere man, and make him into a god."

Then I asked for a few moments to clarify; and she granted me this request. "Kulsum," I said, "Do you believe that Allah has all power?"

Immediately she responded, "Of course, I do. Allah is omnipotent. As Allah wills—that is my creed."

I said, "We, too, believe that Jehovah God is all-powerful. But we do not believe that a man became God. We believe that God who can do anything (I waited until she nodded) can become man if He so chooses. **And all of God that could be 'poured' into a Galilean carpenter was in the One we call Jesus of Nazareth."** Then I commented on the Scripture which tells us the Christ temporarily "set aside" some of His prerogatives and privileges as Deity in order to be "made in human likeness" (PHILIPPIANS 2:7).

Christ is the *"image of the invisible God."* (COLOSSIANS 1:15). I sanction E. Stanley Jones' comment, "If God isn't like Jesus, then frankly I am not interested." The God I know has come to me in Christ Jesus, the perfect reflection of God's grace and glory. God had been speaking through the inspired words of the prophets, priests, and kings of the Old Covenant; but then a new era dawned when the Almighty spoke through the Living Word.

The true and living God has made Himself known in Jesus, His visible image to us earthlings. And it is perilous to reject His conclusive revelation.

PAUL CLARIFIES THIS IN PHILIPPIANS BY SAYING THAT WHEN CHRIST LEFT THE SPLENDORS OF HEAVEN TO COME TO THE SORDIDNESS OF THIS EARTH, HE ASSUMED THE FRAILTY OF HUMAN FLESH. HE WAS THE GOD-MAN, FULLY GOD AND FULLY MAN. AN INSCRUTABLE MYSTERY—YES!

< *FATHER AND SON,*
(*Used by Permission of the Artist Corbert Gauthier*)

"*The Word became flesh and made his dwelling among us. We have seen His glory, the glory of the One and Only, who came from the Father, full of grace and truth.*"
(JOHN 1:14)

BESIDE STILL WATERS >
by Simon Dewey
© Copyright Simon Dewey/
courtesy Altus Fine Art
www.altusfineart.com